SECRET
COLCHESTER

Patrick Denney

AMBERLEY

For Jess

First published 2018

Amberley Publishing
The Hill, Stroud
Gloucestershire, GL5 4EP

www.amberley-books.com

Copyright © Patrick Denney, 2018

The right of Patrick Denney to be identified as the
Author of this work has been asserted in accordance
with the Copyrights, Designs and Patents Act 1988.

ISBN 978 1 4456 7514 5 (print)
ISBN 978 1 4456 7515 2 (ebook)

British Library Cataloguing in Publication Data.
A catalogue record for this book is available from the
British Library.

Origination by Amberley Publishing.
Printed in Great Britain.

Contents

Introduction

The title of this book, *Secret Colchester*, perhaps needs a little explaining. Unlike many books on the history of Colchester, which rightly showcase the very best that the town has to offer including all the major events of the town's history, this book deliberately sets out to take the reader off the beaten track as it were, to the lesser-known and more out of the way places that sometimes tend to get overlooked or forgotten. So, although we shall still be stopping off at a few of the firm favourites, which we may look at from a different angle, we shall also be considering some of the more hidden and obscure aspects of the town's history, but nevertheless of equal interest: buildings, monuments and other places that you may not have given a second glance as you passed them by.

In researching this book I have relied heavily on a wide range of source material including titles such as *The Essex Review* and the *Transactions of the Essex Archaeological Society* as well as delving into numerous old newspapers and other historical reports. I have also spent many happy hours roaming around the streets of Colchester and searching among the roadside verges and undergrowth. I have even resorted to exploring the confines of one or two resident's gardens.

Hopefully this book will appeal to all those with an interest in Colchester – both residents and visitors alike – who wish to add a little more to their knowledge of this fascinating and historical town. I hope that you enjoy reading this book as much as I have enjoyed preparing it.

1. Standing Stones

We are all familiar with the abundance of street furniture that can be seen on our modern highways and footpaths. Items such as road signs, lamp posts, bollards and bus shelters all have their place in our modern world and, of course, all serve a useful purpose. But if you look carefully, you may just spot one or two features that belong to a much earlier period and which are no longer a part of our daily lives.

I'm talking here mainly about stones: small stones, large stones and some stones that look as though they might have been better placed in the local churchyard. By far the most common of these stones that you may come across are what were once used as parish boundary markers. Sometimes these can be seen as isolated examples, perhaps standing on a street corner, or even in the middle of a field somewhere, while others may be grouped together and can be seen running in a line down the side of a street.

Before the local government reforms of the nineteenth century a vast network of parochial parishes extended across the country, controlling virtually every aspect of a person's life such as where they could live, where they could work, where they worshipped and where they could receive support should they fall upon hard times. The rules of each parish applied only to its own parishioners, and they were strictly enforced. For example, if you found yourself in desperate need of help or assistance and happened to live just a foot outside the parish that you were seeking help from, at best you would be ignored and at worst forcibly removed back to the parish to which you legally belonged. As one can imagine, arguments as to parish boundaries and people's rights were commonplace, often having to be settled in a court of law. And so in order to provide some small form of physical structure to what, in reality, was a giant invisible web of hidden boundaries running across the country, it became the custom to fix various forms of boundary markers to provide a permanent reminder as to exactly where a parish boundary was located.

Other standing stones that you may come across once served as milestones or waymarkers. In the days before the availability of large-scale maps, milestones served as a useful point of reference for the traveller whereby one could determine the distance travelled from one point to another. Many of these stones or markers date from around the mid-eighteenth century when, under the various Turnpike Acts, all roads under their jurisdiction were required to have markers erected at 1-mile intervals along a given route – hence the name 'milestones'. Today, many of these old stones have disappeared entirely and those that remain have often suffered from years of neglect: weathering, acts of vandalism, or in some cases fallen foul to modern road-widening schemes. In fact, during the Second World War it was government policy to remove or to bury many of these structures in case they assisted the enemy in the event of an invasion.

In fairly recent times a concerted effort has been made to both record and restore many of these old milestones, with well over 100 survivals having been identified across Essex alone. And thankfully, some of these surviving stones now enjoy 'listed building' status. However, the same is not always the case with regard to parish boundary stones. The problem is that, generally speaking, local authorities are under no real obligation to maintain and preserve these markers unless, of course, they happen to be attached to a listed building. Otherwise they are generally ignored, with at least one or two local examples having disappeared in the last few years alone due to modern development.

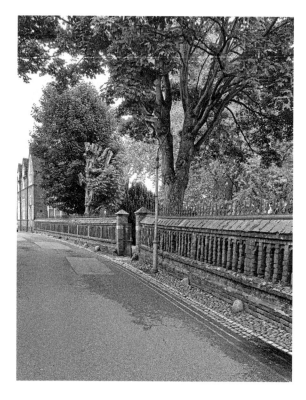

Here we can see a line of twenty parish boundary stones running alongside the wall of St Botolph's Priory, marking the division between the parishes of St James' and St Botolph's. The stones continue in a straight line westwards across St Botolph's Street and into Vineyard Street where another five stones can be seen. It is of interest, however, to note that according to early census records and from an 1848 parish map, the north–south dividing line between the two parishes is actually shown to be around 30 yards (27 metres) to the left of picture, in line with the Roman wall.

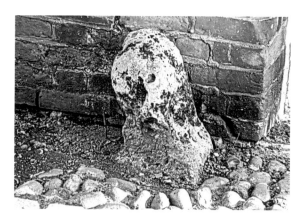

A rather worn-looking boundary marker seen by the entrance to the ruins of St Botolph's Priory.

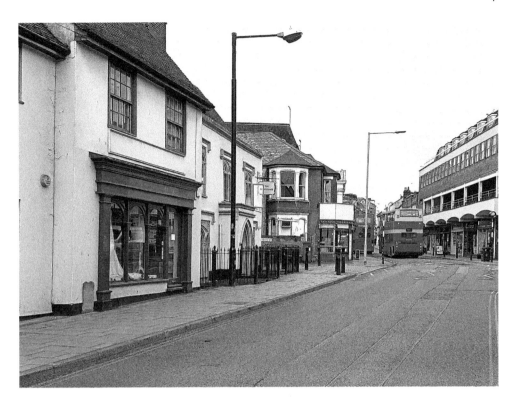

Above: If you look beside the shop window on the left you will see a boundary stone marking the division between St Giles Parish and Holy Trinity Parish.

Right: A close-up view of the parish boundary stone seen above, dated 1849.

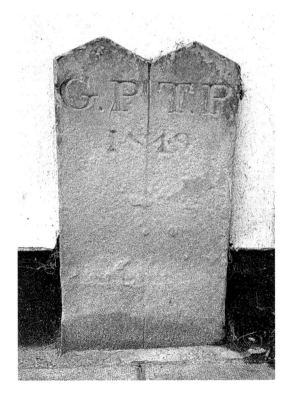

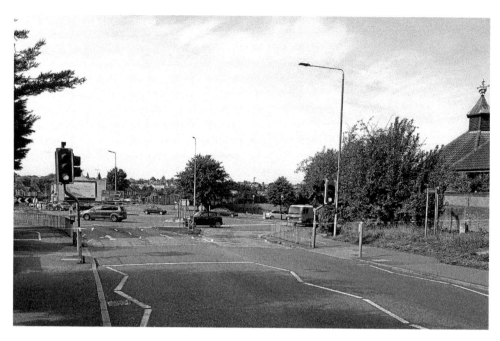

In this 2017 view of Harwich Road looking towards the bypass, you can just see the old Colchester-Harwich milestone standing against the wall on the right side of the road. According to John Ogilby's London to Harwich travel map of 1675, this was the 52-mile point between London and Harwich.

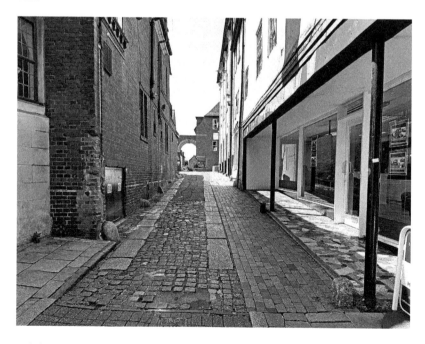

More parish boundary stones can be seen here, running either side of Balkerne Passage and marking the boundary between St Peter's and St Mary's parishes.

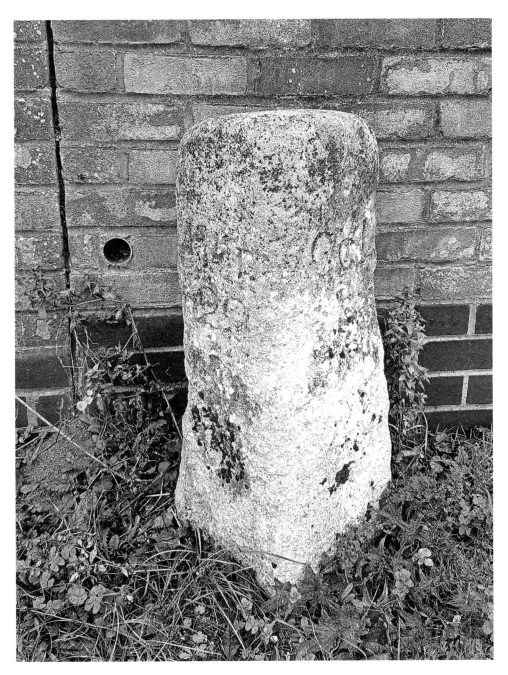

A close-up of the milestone seen opposite shows that the traveller is 20 miles away from Harwich and 1 mile away from Colchester. It would appear that the stone has been moved on at least two occasions: when the old bypass was constructed in the early 1930s and when further improvements were made to this junction in more recent years. In fact, on a personal note, I can remember sitting and climbing on this stone many times while growing up in the area in the 1950s. In those days the stone was positioned much closer to the footpath at the bottom of a steep grass bank.

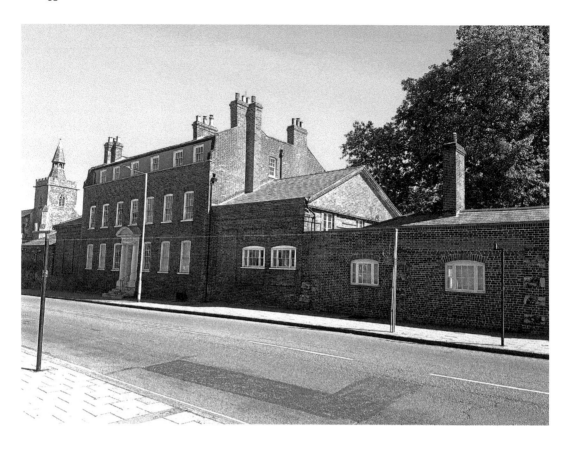

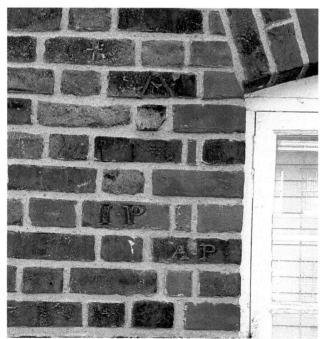

Above: The division between the boundary of St James' and All Saints' parishes in the lower High Street is interesting in that it runs directly through a building, which must have caused some problems for the parish officers in deciding how the parish rates should be apportioned. The division between the two parishes runs just to the left of the right-hand window, in line with the chimney stack.

Left: A close-up view of the brickwork showing the initials of both St James' and All Saints' parishes.

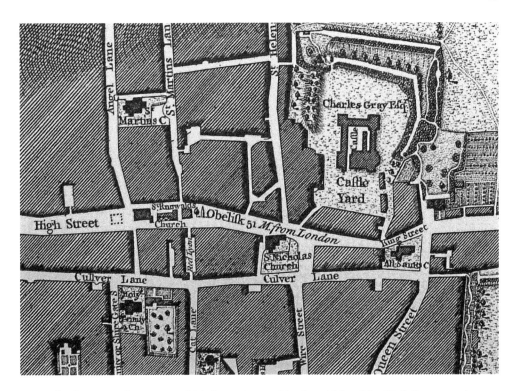

One rather large standing stone, which formerly stood in the middle of the High Street, was known as the obelisk and served as quite a spectacular-looking milestone. On this detail from Chapman and André's 1777 map of Colchester, it shows the obelisk standing on the 51-mile mark from London. In 1858, after deciding to remove the obelisk from the High Street, it was auctioned off on-site and sold for £3 5s (£3.25). The purchaser was Charles Wire, who removed the stone on the following day and later transferred it to the cemetery in Mersea Road. It later became a memorial stone for his wife Ann, who died in June 1859.

The obelisk was first installed in the High Street in 1760 as an ornamental milestone recording the distances between Colchester, London, Norwich and other towns. It was set up by Charles Gray on behalf of the Turnpike Trustees at a total cost of £4 7s (£4.35). This included 10s and sixpence (52½p) paid to James Deane for the design, £3 6s (£3.30) paid to Ben Barnes, the stonemason, and another 10s and sixpence paid to Mr Brand for 'painting and lettering it'. The fact that the letters were painted onto the obelisk suggests that they were not actually carved into the stone. This might suggest that when it was later turned into a memorial stone the existing letters may simply have been cleaned off before the new carving of the letters took place. The other possibility that has been suggested is that the stone panels were reversed and the memorial inscription was then carved onto a fresh blank surface. It has also been suggested that the obelisk itself may not have been constructed from scratch in 1760, but rather adapted from a previous structure that once stood further down the High Street – somewhere near the top of East Hill in All Saints' parish.

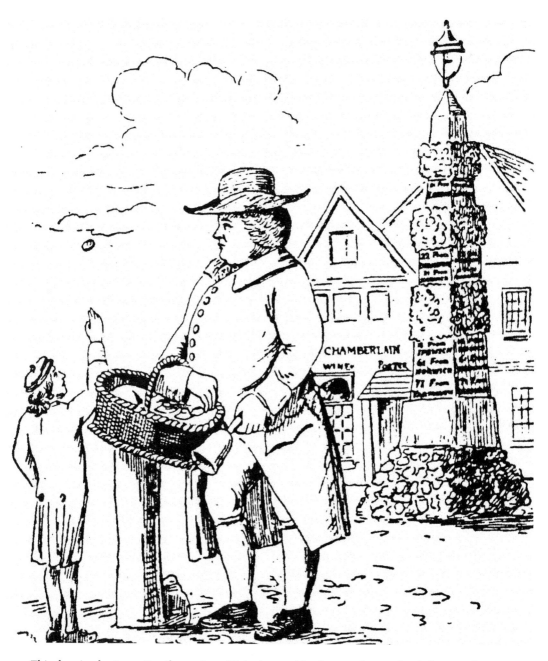

This drawing by James Dunthorne Jr, published on 12 March 1792, shows a local character known as 'the Pie Man' standing in front of the obelisk in the High Street. Apparently, in order to boost his sales, the Pie Man used to offer the boys from the Bluecoat School a free pie if they could win two out of three coin tosses.

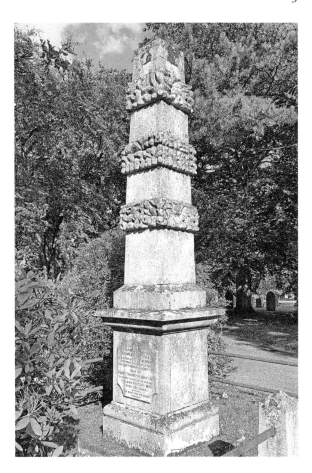

The obelisk as it looks today.

A close-up of the panel explaining the stone's origins and its subsequent dedication to Mary Ann Wire.

2. 'Jurassic Park'

If you thought that you needed to travel to the south of England in order to search for ancient fossils along the Jurassic Coast, then think again. You need go no further than Colchester's very own Castle Park to view what appear to be some fine examples of ammonite imprints preserved in the town's Roman wall.

Most of the stone that comprises the Roman wall, along with the Roman brick itself, is known as septaria, which is a form of fossilised mud derived from the underlying London clay of Essex that outcrops around the coastal districts of Harwich and Wrabness. It is thought that the Romans quarried large amounts of this stone for use in their various building projects – including the town's Roman wall. But herewith we have a bit of a problem. Because most of the fossil imprints discovered in the town wall appear to be ammonites, a long extinct marine creature that existed during the Jurassic period (*c.* 200–145 million years ago), then what are they doing in the Roman wall which is built mainly of septaria nodules from the London clay and which date from the much more recent Eocene period (*c.* 56–34 million years ago). The short answer is that the septarian nodules containing these ammonite imprints must be different from most of the other nodules in the wall. In fact, these specimens may have derived from boulder clay deposits originating somewhat to the north of Essex, which were later brought south during the glacial movements of the ice age. It is well known that these boulder clay deposits are a rich source of marine fossils – including ammonites.

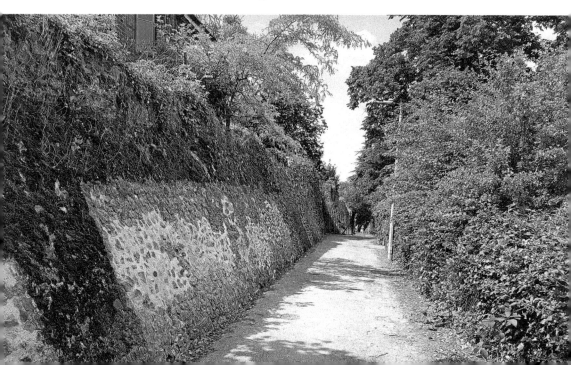

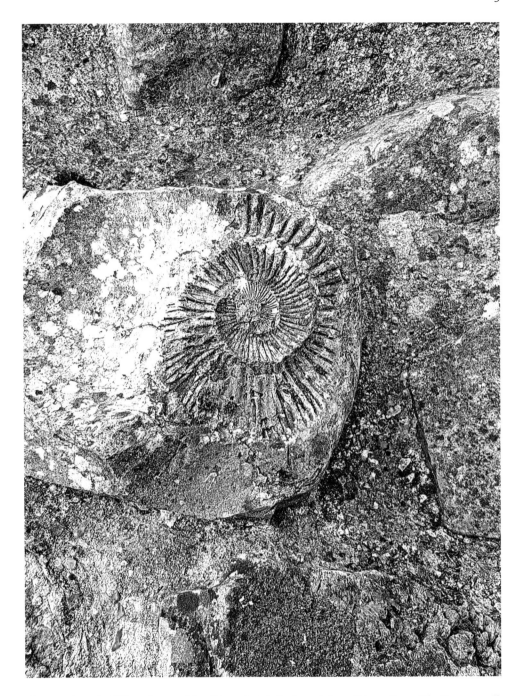

Above and overleaf: Two of several fossil imprints to be found along this section of the Roman wall.

Opposite: The footpath running alongside the Roman wall in Lower Castle Park.

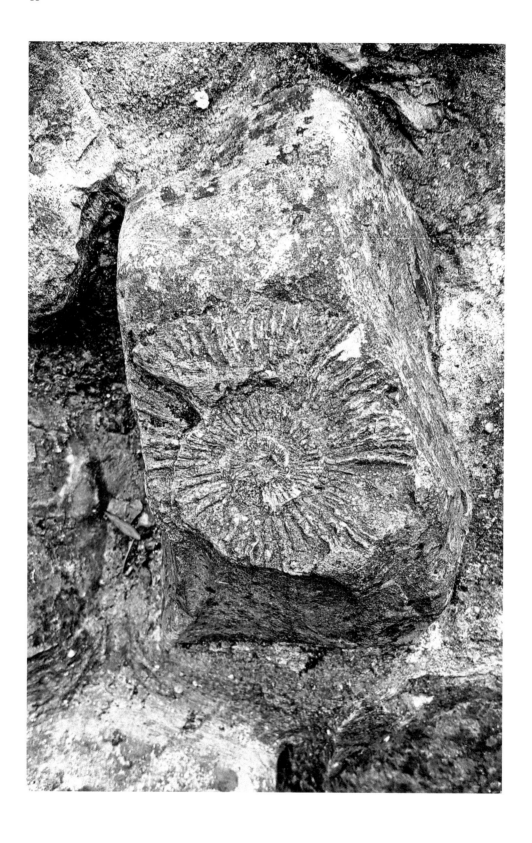

3. The Colchester Stop Line

Following the hasty retreat from Dunkirk in late May and early June of 1940, immediate plans were put in place by the government to prepare for a possible invasion. It was thought that a German invasion of England was likely to happen sooner rather than later and that any attack by enemy forces would likely involve the landing of large numbers of troops and equipment somewhere along the east and south coasts. Apart from bolstering the coastal defences in these areas, a rapid construction of defensive fortifications took place in a very short period of time, turning much of the country into a temporary battlefield.

By September 1940, hundreds of miles of anti-tank ditches had been dug and around 18,000 pillboxes and other defensive structures had been built. Major roads and river crossings were protected with lines of reinforced concrete blocks and other obstacles, many of which were also supported by additional rifle and machine gun positions with the primary purpose being to halt, or at least slow down, the advance of the enemy.

The main anti-tank line of fortifications to protect London itself and the industrial towns of the Midlands was known as the General Headquarters Line (GHQ Line), which ran across southern England before skirting London and then running north from the Thames Estuary to its intended destination at Edinburgh, although much of this northern section was never actually completed. But because the coastal areas of Essex were deemed to be a likely landing place for enemy forces, a secondary line of defence was established much nearer to the coast known as the Eastern Command Line. This followed the River Colne in Essex from a position near Fingringhoe, then ran north around Colchester and on to the Chappel Viaduct and to Mount Bures before heading into Suffolk and Norfolk. However, to most local people this was simply known as the 'Colchester Stop Line'. In fact, because of the town's strategic importance, it was also decided to turn Colchester itself into an anti-tank island, effectively surrounding the town with anti-tank defences and other fortifications.

Although much of this extensive anti-tank barrier around the town followed natural obstacles, such as the river and other ditches and embankments, particularly to the north and east of the town, it was nevertheless necessary to dig a massive ditch some 4 miles in length across the town's southern and western boundaries. This ran from the Lexden side of town before crossing Shrub End Road, Layer Road, Berechurch Road, Mersea Road, Middlewick Ranges and finally Old Heath Road before running down to the marshes and to the River Colne. On some stretches of this route it was possible to incorporate some of the surviving ancient ramparts that date from the Iron Age period, originally constructed as anti-chariot traps. The ditch itself was probably around 15 feet wide and 10 feet deep, and each road crossing would have been protected by various other defences including concrete roadblocks and gun emplacements. While very few of these fortifications still survive today they haven't disappeared altogether, as can be seen from the following examples.

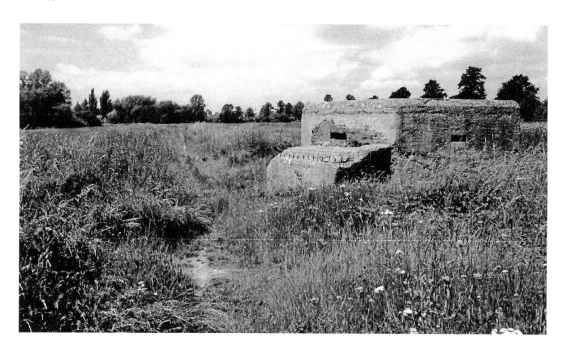

A solid-looking Second World War pillbox sited in a meadow alongside Cowdray Avenue, near the River Colne, *c.* 1980. The entrance to the pillbox was on the left of the building as seen and was partially protected by a blast wall, which has received some damage to the top here.

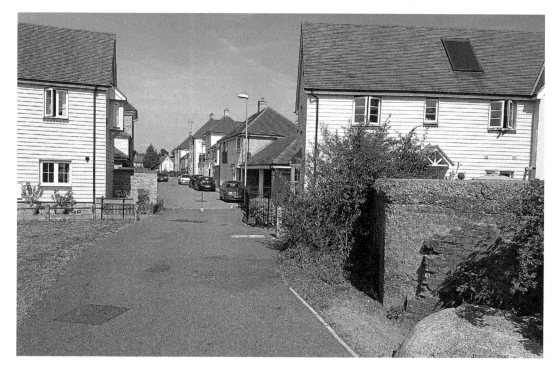

The same pillbox today (partially visible on the right), now standing in the middle of a modern housing estate.

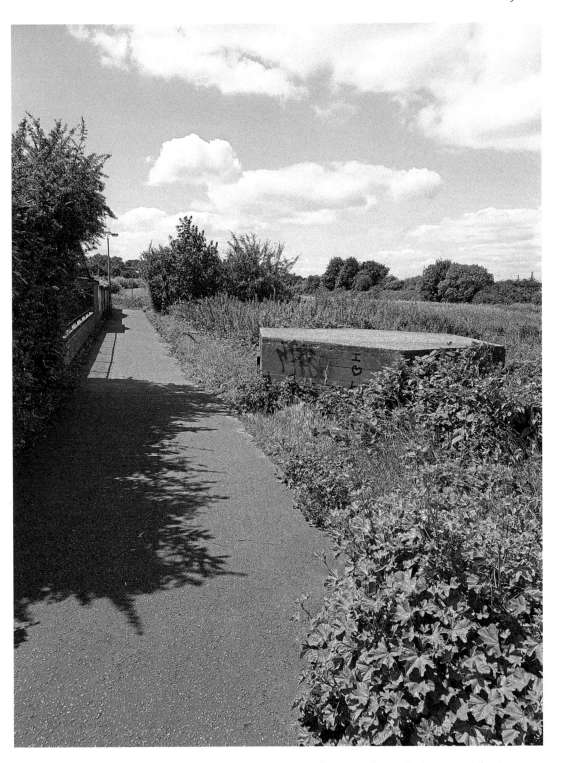

This pillbox can be seen standing next to the footpath that runs alongside the River Colne just south of Hythe railway station.

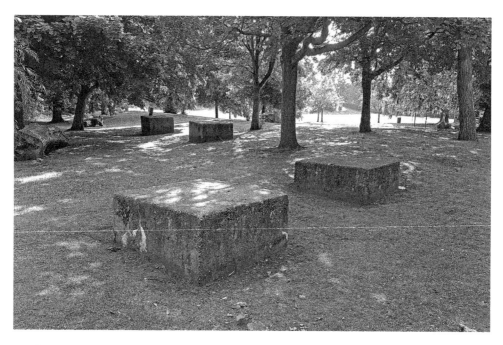

No, these are not modern sculptures set to enhance this area of Castle Park, but the remains of an anti-tank defence system along the River Colne. The four concrete blocks seen here were positioned at a potential crossing on the river and were joined together with thick steel cables, thereby making an effective barrier. Each block is in the form of a cube partly sunk into the ground, with all sides measuring 5 feet in length (152 cm).

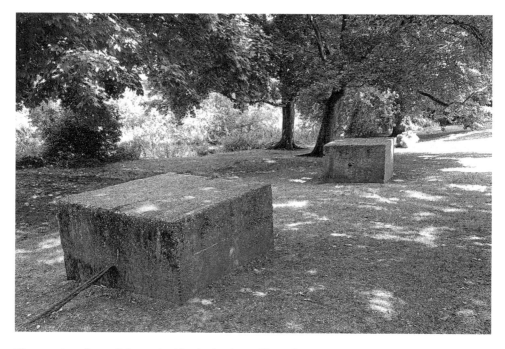

The remains of one of the steel cables is clearly visible in this view.

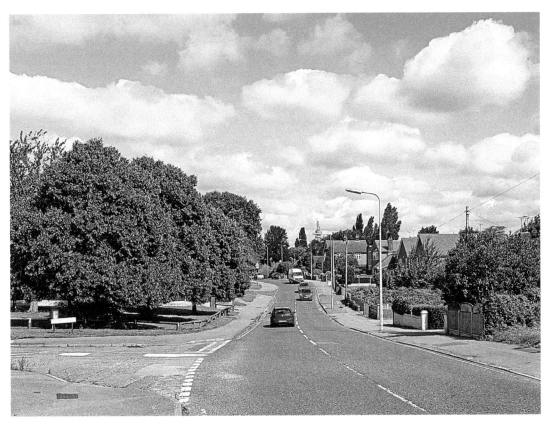

This stretch of Old Heath Road, near to its junction with Speedwell Road, looks fairly peaceful today, but during the Second World War this approach into town was heavily defended with an array of anti-tank blocks and ditches. Based on official records, as well as from the recollections of a number of Old Heath residents, we can begin to piece together a picture of how it may have looked.

For a start, 'crossing the road' at a point somewhere between the blue and red cars in the picture, ran an anti-tank ditch. This was part of the 4-mile-long ditch that ran from the River Colne right across the southern side of Colchester. Keith Moss, an Old Heath resident, can recall there being a deep ditch dug and filled with water, running from the Old Heath Road across the playing field (seen on the left beneath the trees) towards the Wick.

On the right side of the road, just inside what was then a farmer's field (now the front gardens of a row of houses), was a row of sixteen concrete blocks – some of which still survive. At the edge of the playing field on the left were a series of concrete 'pimples' – smaller pyramid-type stone obstacles designed to prevent tanks passing over.

Across the main road were some permanent concrete blocks, which had sufficient space in the middle to allow traffic to pass. In the centre of the road were some steel plates (approximately 18 square inches, or 45 cm) into which bent steel railway girders could be inserted when necessary. Keith Moss remembers that his father had to practise fitting these rail girders into the metal plates as part of his Home Guard duties.

Finally, there was a row of concrete blocks running across the entrance to Speedwell Road, seen on the left. Local resident Gladys Rudd, who lived in a house just inside the road, remembers that they used to enjoy playing on the blocks as children, jumping from one to the other. Gladys can also remember that in the rear garden of No. 287 Old Heath Road, which was directly opposite her front door, there was a trench dug that was manned by either soldiers or members of the Home Guard, who had a crate of bottles in the form of Molitov cocktails ready to defend the tank trap.

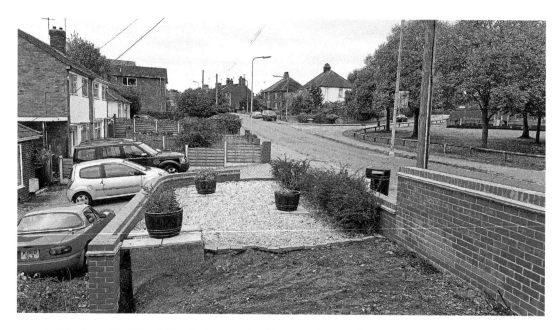

In this view of Old Heath Road looking in the direction of Rowhedge, one of the surviving concrete anti-tank blocks can be seen beneath a black plant container in the garden of No. 364 Old Heath Road. The block is again in the form of a cube, partly buried and with sides measuring 3 feet 6 inches (107 cm).

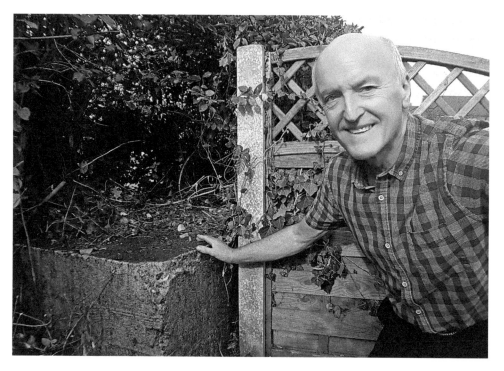

Here we have another view from the front garden of No. 370 Old Heath Road, showing one of two surviving concrete blocks that once formed part of the anti-tank defence system.

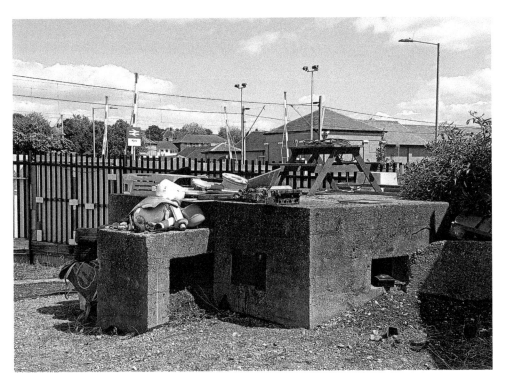

This pillbox, which is now completely hidden from view in Hythe Station Road, was positioned to protect the nearby railway crossing.

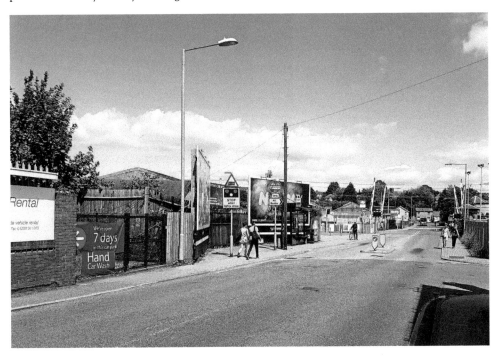

Hythe Station Road with the pillbox obscured behind the hoardings on the left.

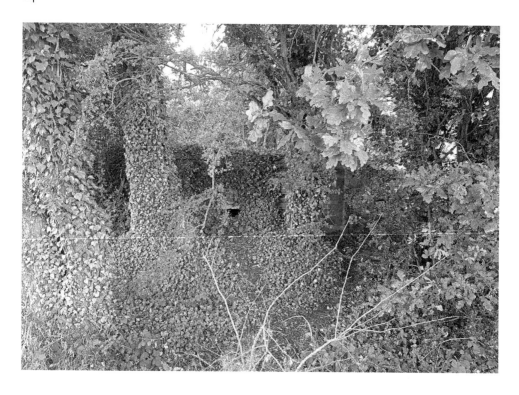

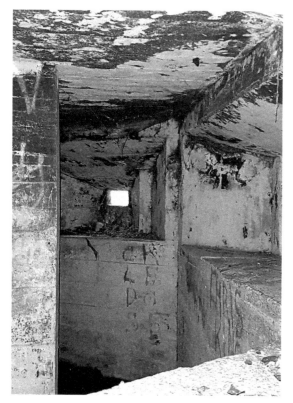

Above: If you look carefully you can just see the peephole of this pillbox located on Middlewick, which is otherwise completly covered in foliage. This pillbox was sited to protect the anti-tank ditch mentioned above (*see* page 21)

Left: An interior view of the pillbox on Middlewick.

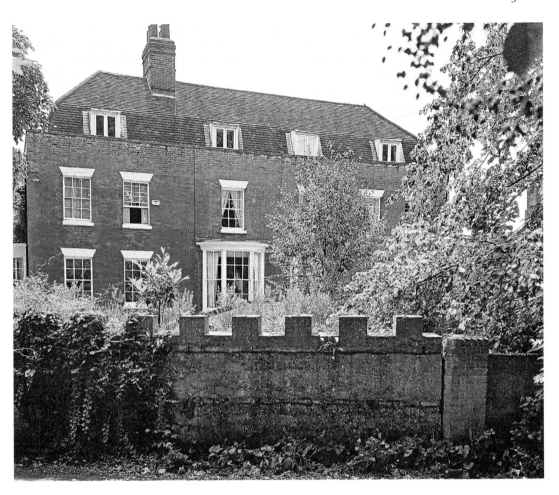

This is the front garden wall of East Bay House, which incorporates a built-in firing post, complete with crenulations. The wall is made of concrete and is 33 feet long, 5 feet high and over 2 feet thick. Apparently it is the only example of its kind in Essex, so is a rare survival. If you look carefully you can see where wooden battens were once affixed to the wall, which in turn would have supported a wooden fence, thus helping to disguise its position. The firing post would have been well placed to help protect the vital river crossing at this location.

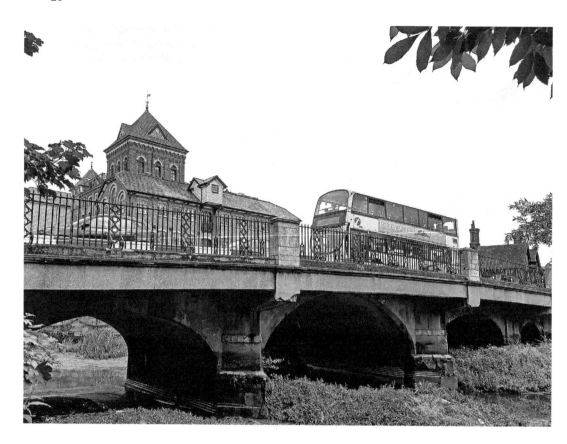

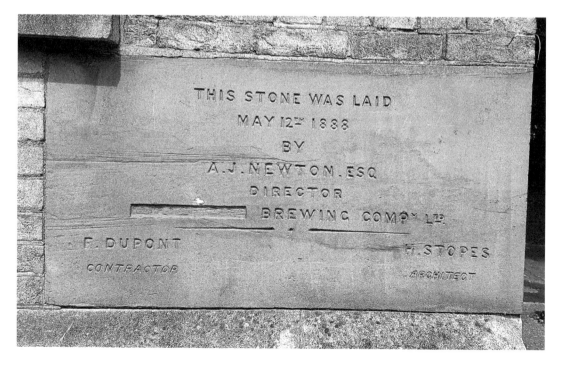

THIS STONE WAS LAID
MAY 12TH 1888
BY
A.J. NEWTON. ESQ
DIRECTOR
BREWING COMPY LTD

F. DUPONT

CONTRACTOR

H. STOPES

ARCHITECT

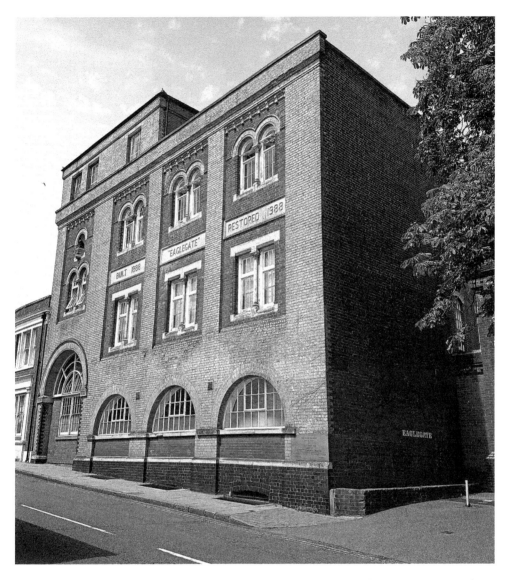

Above: In an attempt to hinder the enemy's advancement it was decided to remove, or at least disguise, any identifying marks such as place names or street signs. An example of this can be seen on the foundation stone of what was once the Colchester Brewing Co. on East Hill. In the event that the enemy had successfully crossed East Bridge, and assuming that they wouldn't have known where they were (which is extremely unlikely), the name 'Colchester' was physically erased from the foundation stone. However, this would have been a rather futile attempt to disguise the enemy's position because just a few hundred yards up East Hill they would have found the war memorial with the name 'Colchester' emblazed in bronze on the name plate – not to mention, of course, the famous Norman castle standing right in front of them.

Opposite above: East Bridge as seen from the position of the firing post.

Opposite below: The foundation stone on the Colchester Brewing Co. showing where the name 'Colchester' has been erased from the title.

4. 'Royal' Postboxes

Wherever you travel around the British Isles you will never be too far away from the distinctive red-coloured postbox, and latest figures would suggest that there are more than 115,000 of them of currently in existence. The earliest postboxes in this country date from 1852 and although they were initially painted red, as they are today, they were subsequently painted a kind of bronze-green colour, which was to become the norm up until 1874. At this time it was decided to revert back to the original red colour, although it would take around ten years before all the existing boxes were repainted.

The boxes themselves came in various shapes and designs but were all basically classified as either pillar boxes, wall boxes, lamp boxes or Ludlow boxes, the latter of which were exclusively used for sub-post offices. Most of the boxes also incorporated the royal cipher in its design and whenever a new sovereign acceded to the throne, a new cipher was used on the box. So, from the 1850s right through to the present day, the royal ciphers of six sovereigns have been incorporated into the design of all postboxes. In theory, therefore, it should be possible, in most cases, to track the development of a local community from its historic centre outwards to its later urban development, simply by taking note of the royal ciphers on the postboxes. The only exception to this rule would have been during the period 1879–87, when the royal cipher and the words 'Post Office' were omitted from all boxes. These were known as 'anonymous boxes' and only around 300 survive from the period. A further identifying mark relating to these anonymous boxes – constructed from 1883 onwards – was that the posting aperture, which had previously been placed right at the top of the box just under the rim, was then lowered several inches further down to prevent the letters getting trapped at the top of the box. And so, with regard to these anonymous boxes, it is fairly easy to identify those that were constructed either before or after 1883 depending on where the posting aperture is positioned.

At the time of writing, the records would indicate that there are something in the order of 107 postboxes currently in use in the central area of Colchester, excluding the outlying districts, among which are a number of fairly rare examples dating from the 1880s.

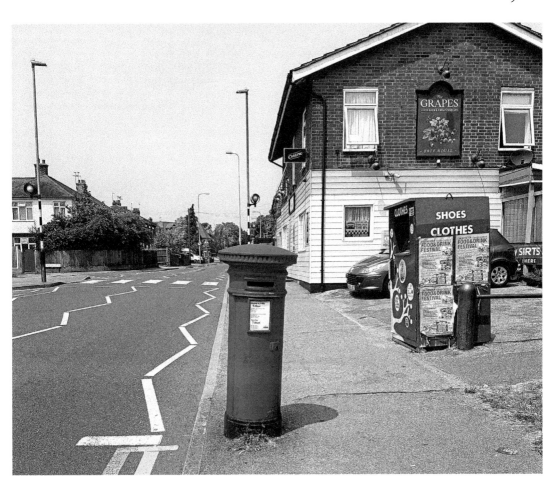

This so-called anonymous postbox seen outside the Grapes public house in Mersea Road is one of only three such boxes in Colchester. It is 'anonymous' in that it lacks the royal cipher and the words 'Post Office' either side of the posting aperture. In 1879–87 these markings were mistakenly omitted from the castings and were only reintroduced afterwards. We can, however, be a little more precise as to the date of this box because from 1879 to 1883 the posting aperture was located right at the top of the box, immediately below the rim. This caused some letters and packages to get stuck at the top of the box and remain unseen by the postmen, so from 1883 the aperture was lowered a few inches further down. So as our box has its posting aperture in the lower position it must date from sometime between 1883 and 1887.

The other two examples, which can be seen in Creffield Road and Lexden Road, are of the same period and collectively are the oldest postboxes in Colchester.

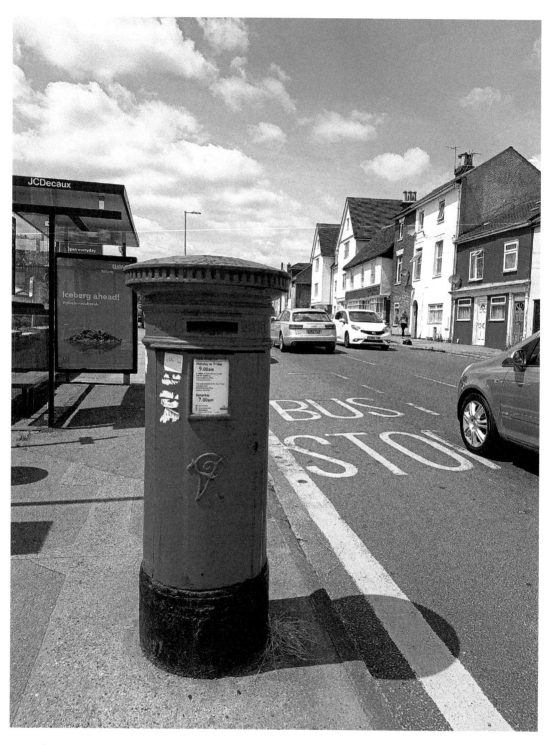

This Victorian postbox bearing the 'VR' monogram of Queen Victoria is located in Magdalen Street. The royal cipher, together with the words 'Post Office' either side of the letter aperture, date this box to sometime after 1887.

Right: At first sight this appears to be a rather strange location for this George VI postbox in Athelstan Road. It certainly seems unusual that the Post Office would place a postbox within the confines of someone's property boundary. However, as the next picture will show, this house was formerly a sub Post Office.

Below: Here is No. 19 Athelstan Road, pictured in the early years of the twentieth century when the premises incorporated a sub-Post Office run by Charles Frost. The house, which dates from around 1903, included an Edward VII Ludlow-type postbox on the property boundary. These boxes were so named from a design by James Ludlow in 1885 and were used almost exclusively for sub-Post Offices until the firm's closure in 1965. The boxes, which were usually made of wood and designed to fit within a wall rather than freestanding, often incorporated a distinctive enamel plate bearing the royal cipher and the words 'Post Office Letter Box'.

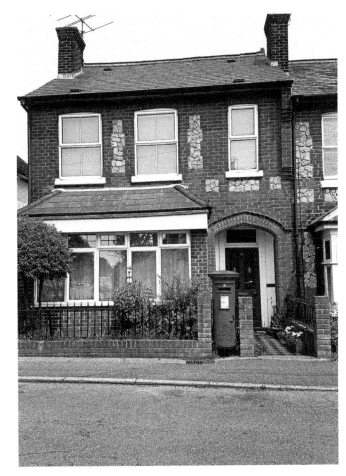

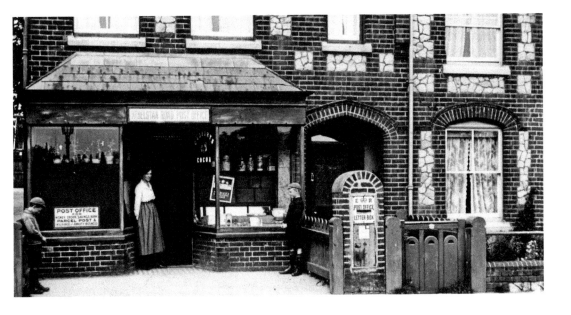

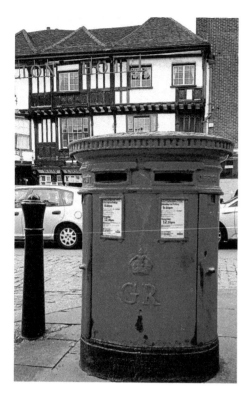

This larger-capacity double-aperture box is seen in Colchester High Street opposite the Red Lion Hotel. The royal cipher on the front of the box tells us that it dates from the reign of George V (1910–36).

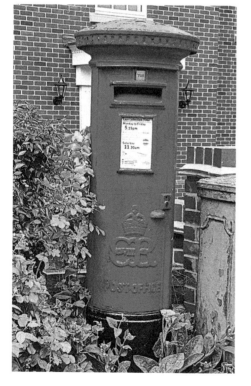

The rarest postbox in Colchester is this example in Glen Avenue, which dates from 1936 and carries the royal cipher of Edward VIII. Edward VIII only reigned for 325 days – between January and December 1936 – so relatively few postboxes were commissioned during this period. In fact, only 271 postboxes were manufactured nationwide, of which just 161 were the standard pillar boxes – only around 150 of these survive today.

5. Churches, Chapels and Burials

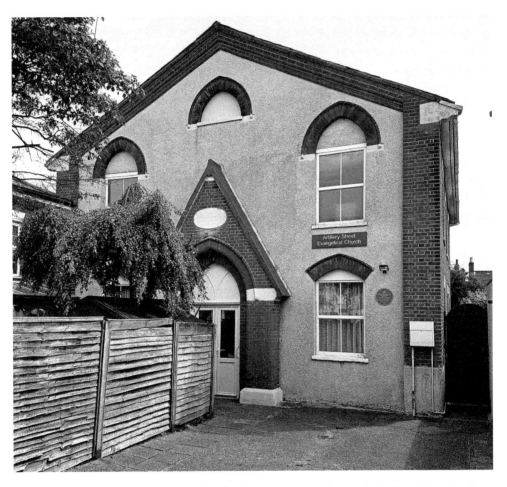

This former Primitive Methodist chapel, set back among a row of houses in Artillery Street, is where the well-known nineteenth-century Baptist preacher and evangeliser Charles Haddon Spurgeon is said to have found salvation. The event is reported to have occurred one snowy Sunday morning in January 1850 after setting off from his home on Hythe Hill to attend a religious meeting elsewhere. The weather was proving to be extremely bad, so he decided to turn off into a side street and found himself stepping inside this chapel. He was so moved by the experience that he became convinced that the truth was more likely to be found among the poorer and humble members of society rather than the more refined and educated. Just a few months later, on 3 May, he was baptised at Iseham Ferry in Cambridgeshire. In 1854 he became the pastor of the New Park Street Chapel in London, later moving to the new Metropolitan Chapel where he remained for thirty-eight years until his death in 1892 at the age of fifty-seven years.

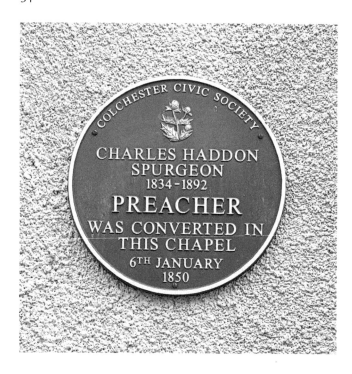

A commemorative plaque dedicated to Charles Haddon Spurgeon erected by the Colchester Civic Society.

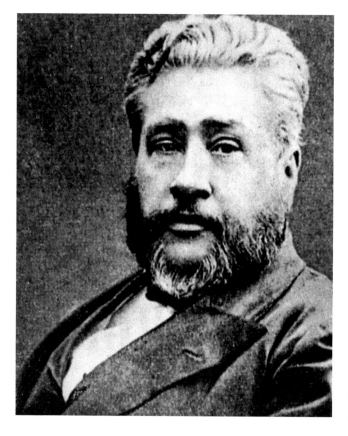

Charles Haddon Spurgeon, pictured in later life.

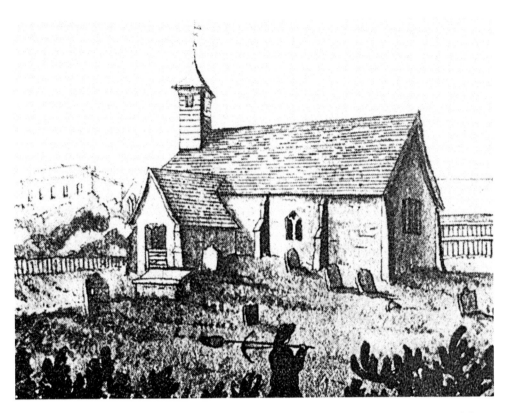

This view shows the old church of St Michael's at Mile End (Myland), which was pulled down following the building of the new church in the 1850s. Only the ruins of the old building now survive in Rectory Close. The church was located around a mile from the town centre, which may account for the name 'Mile End'. It had become increasingly obvious in the early 1850s that the church was no longer fit for purpose and the rector at the time, Archibald Julius, noted in the 1851 religious census, 'A new church is in contemplation as many persons leave the church every Sunday, not being able to find a seat.' In fact, the official attendance recorded on 30 March 1851 revealed that 123 adults and fifty-three Sunday scholars attended the morning service and 197 adults and fifty-three Sunday scholars attended the afternoon service, which by today's standards doesn't seem too bad! The maximum accommodation of the church comprised 250 sittings, 240 of which were free, with the remaining ten sittings being available at a cost of £2 each.

Ann Gilbert (née Taylor), sister to Jane Taylor of 'Twinkle Twinkle Little Star' fame, wrote of her time living in Angel lane (now West Stockwell Street) and described the view from the workshop at the rear of the house: 'Happy years I have spent in that shabby old room. From the window we could just see over the garden, and beyond the roofs, Mile End church and Parsonage in the pretty distance, reminding us of the evening walk which usually followed the day's work.'

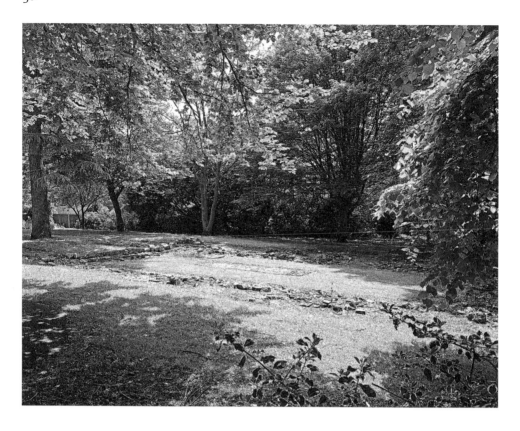

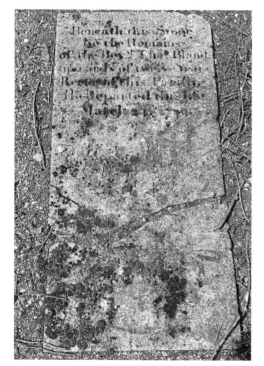

Above: The ruins of the old church.

Left: This surviving tombstone is dedicated to the memory of Thomas Bland, a former rector of the parish. It reads, 'Beneath this stone lie the remains of the Revd Thos Bland upwards of 12 years Rector of this Parish who departed this life March 24th 1789.'

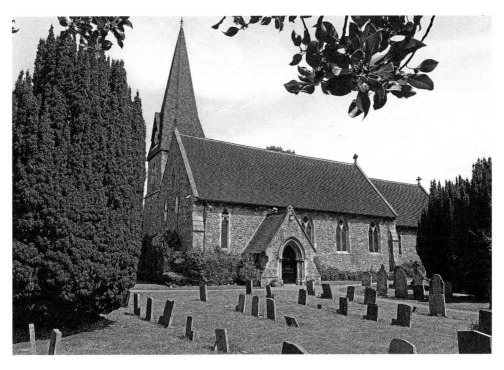

The modern church of St Michael's, Mile End, which was consecrated on 18 May 1855.

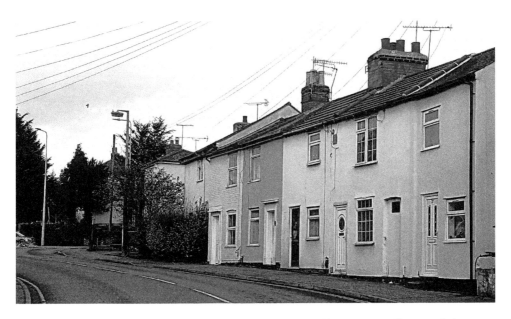

In this view of Lower Harwich Road looking up towards the old bypass you will note a slight recess between two of the houses on the right and a plaque or sign fixed to the wall. This marks the site of the Holy Well, long since associated with St Anne's Chapel, which stood on this site from ancient times until around the eighteenth century, by which time it had been converted into a barn. The chapel was known to exist from at least 1344 and was associated with a hermitage.

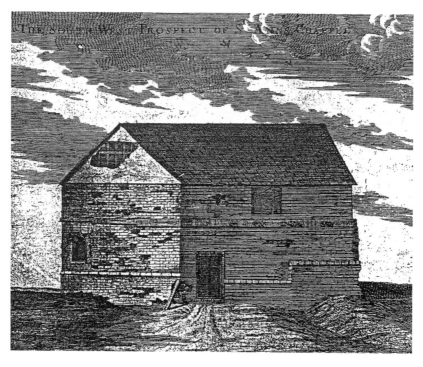

The remains of St Anne's Chapel as seen from John Pryor's *Prospect of Colchester* (1724).

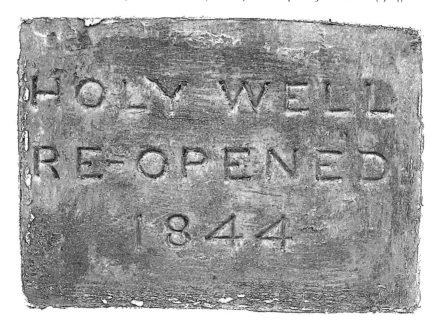

This stone commemorates the reopening of the Holy Well in 1844. According to a Colchester guidebook published in 1897 the well was still being used at this time. It states, 'The well is still in existence, an excellent legacy to the poor of the district and still called Holy Well.' A later guidebook, published in 1922, again states that the well was still being used, although by later years it appears to have been resealed.

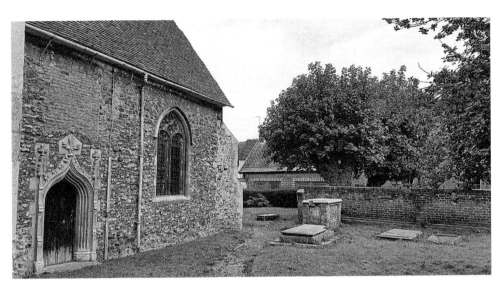

In this view of St Martin's churchyard note the gravestone to the far right of the picture. This marks the resting place of Jacob Ringer, a Dutch baymaker who departed this life in January 1681. This is the only tangible evidence to be seen locally that a bay trade actually existed in the town (bay being a type of cloth). In reality, of course, baymaking was one of the town's major industries between around 1565 and 1830 and brought much prosperity to the area.

To add to the interest of the grave, we know that Jacob Ringer lived during the turbulent years of the Siege of Colchester during the Civil War, and following the surrender of the town he was obliged to pay £10 (at least £20,000 in today's money, based on average earnings) towards the total fine of £10,000 imposed on the town by Parliament, a sum that itself was perhaps equivalent to as much £20 million in today's money.

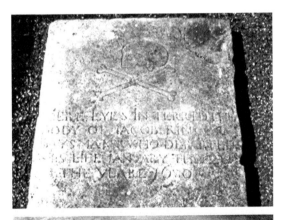

The tombstone of Jacob Ringer. Note the skull and crossbones at the head of the tombstone: a common emblem at the time known as a *memento mori*, a reminder of the assured expectation of death.

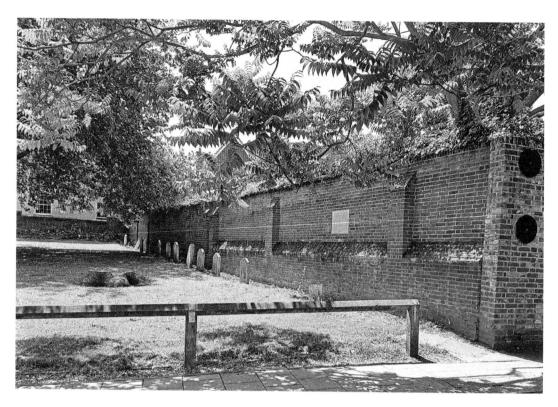

From 1778 until 1853 this plot of land, adjacent to St Helen's Chapel in St Helen's Lane, was used as a graveyard by the Society of Friends (Quakers) until being acquired by the council in 1952. At this time the remaining tombstones, representing at least 200 burials over the period, were moved to the side walls. The brick wall seen to the right of the plot containing the stone plaque, although since demolished and rebuilt, once formed part of the boundary wall of an old Independent meeting house that stood on the adjacent site from around 1693 until 1895 when it was demolished and the land used to extend the playground of the neighbouring Bluecoat School. It may also be of interest to note that the meeting house in question was where Isaac Taylor, father of Ann and Jane Taylor, served as minister between 1796 and 1810 (*see* page 35).

Another interesting event concerning the old meeting house took place in 1816. The minister at the time, Joseph Herrick, had fallen out of favour with some of the chapel's trustees and in order to prevent him from preaching there any longer they removed the roof of the building, thereby forcing him to move elsewhere.

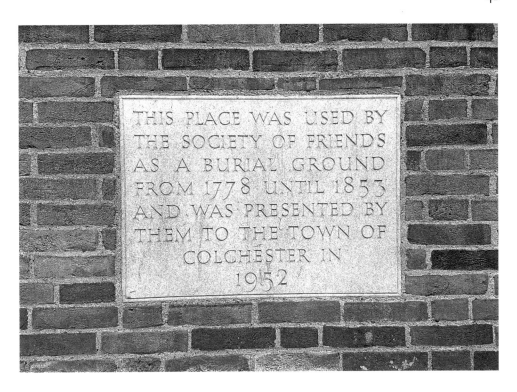

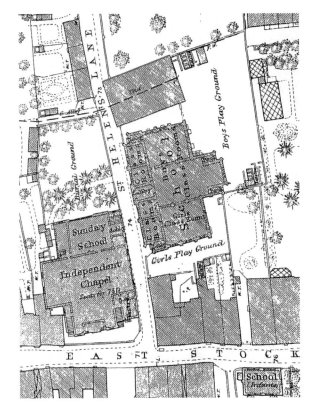

Above: A stone tablet built into part of the boundary wall of the former old meeting house.

Right: A detail from the 1876 Ordnance Survey map showing the old meeting house still standing on the boundary of the Quaker burial ground – note the red line marking the surviving boundary wall.

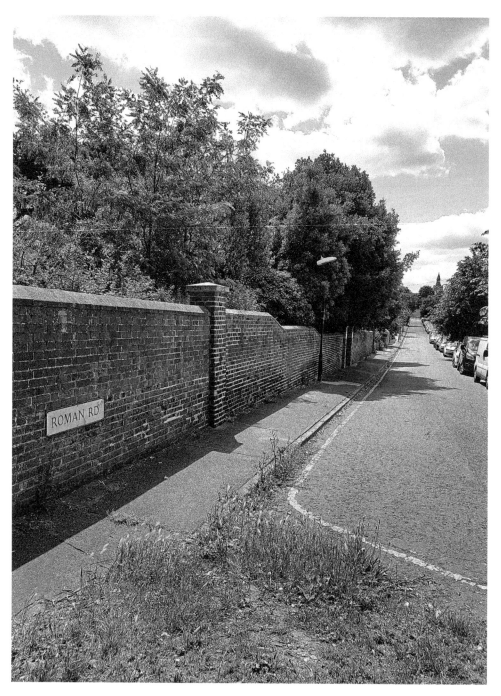

In this quiet corner of Roman Road, behind the wall on the left and almost tucked away from prying eyes, lies a burial ground belonging to the Society of Friends. From around 1823, the surrounding land had been transformed into a large botanical garden that had been created in the north-east corner of the walled town by the Botanical and Horticultural Society. However, by 1851 the venture had failed and the land was sold off for development. The Society of Friends managed to purchase four of the plots, utilising three of them for use as a burial ground.

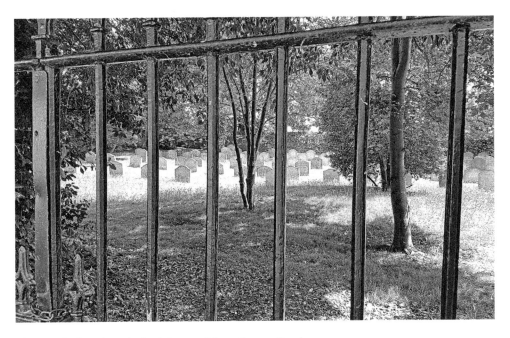

The view looking into the burial ground from Roman Road.

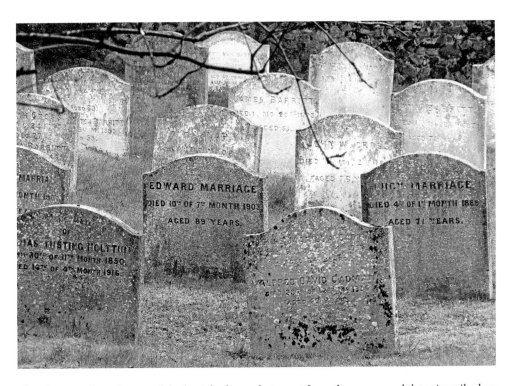

This close-up view of some of the burials shows that apart from the names and dates inscribed on the individual stones they are almost all the same, reinforcing the belief that there should be no distinction between rich and poor – even in death.

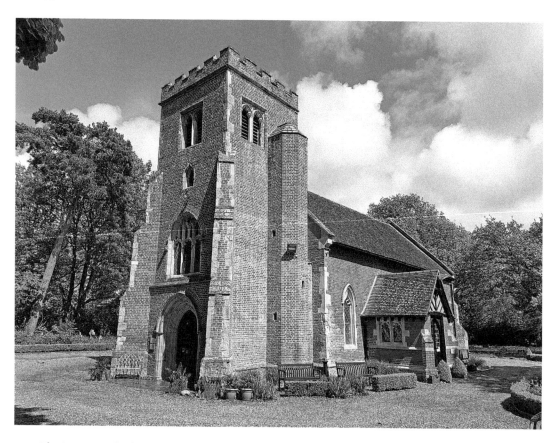

The impressive-looking red-brick Church of St Michael's at Berechurch (West Donyland) was rebuilt from an earlier structure around 1500. The church was originally a chapel of ease to Holy Trinity in Colchester, but after the Dissolution of the Monasteries in 1536 it came into the possession of the Audley family and their successors, who also owned the nearby Berechurch Hall. A large part of the building, including the nave and chancel, were rebuilt in 1872 and although the church was declared redundant in 1975 and turned into office accommodation, the former Audley chapel still survives intact and is open to the public.

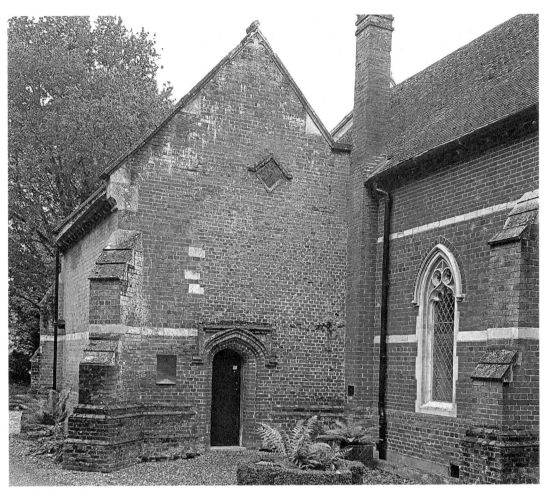

The Audley chapel, which is attached to the north-east corner of the church, was probably added sometime after 1536 when Sir Thomas Lord Audley was granted the church and estate from the Crown following the Dissolution of the Monasteries. He subsequently had parochial status conferred upon the church, although this may have happened sometime earlier. Sir Thomas was born at Earls Colne and eventually went on to become town clerk of Colchester, Speaker of the House of Commons and ultimately Lord Chancellor of England, and in 1538 was raised to the peerage as Baron Audley of Walden. However, returning to the Audley chapel at Berechurch, nothing can quite prepare the modern visitor for what lies inside the rather ordinary-looking red-brick Tudor doorway.

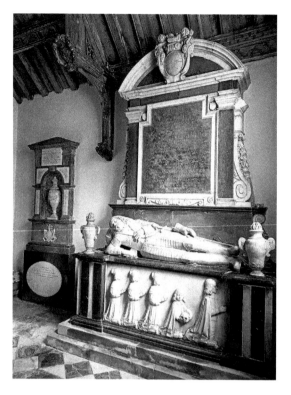

This view taken from inside the chapel hardly does it justice, but perhaps gives an impression of the richly decorated interior. Of particular prominence is the imposing memorial monument of Sir Henry Audley, who was the great-grand-nephew of Sir Thomas Lord Audley. He had his memorial created in 1648, some years before his own death sometime after 1664. The tomb shows the effigy of Sir Henry in a reclining position dressed in the armour-clad uniform of a knight, below which his five children can be seen – Katherine, Marian, Abigail, Henry and Thomas. One of the sons, presumably Henry, is seen holding a skull in his hands, indicating that he died before the erection of the monument. Above the tomb is a large transcription in the form of a reredos, surmounted by a segmental pediment containing a cartouche that would once have included his painted coat of arms.

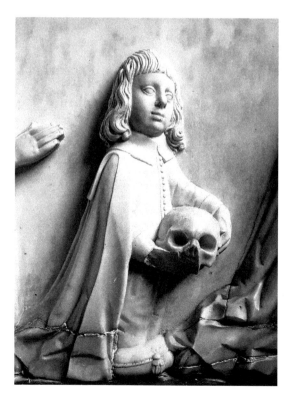

Detail showing one of the figures on the front of the tomb.

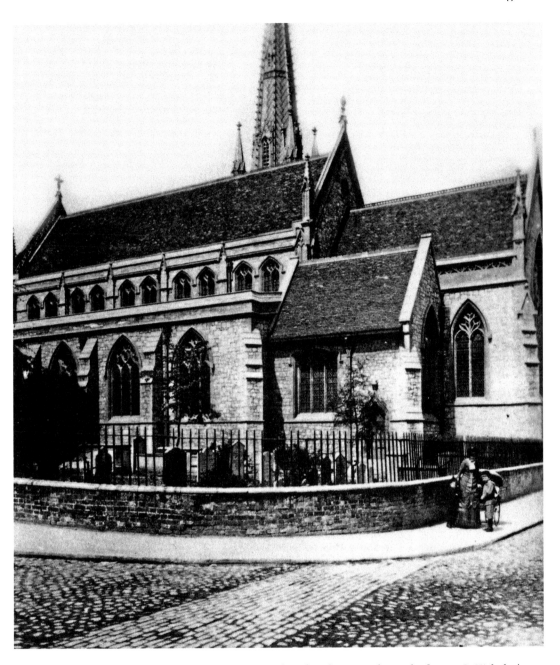

Although probably unrecognisable to many people today, this view shows the former St Nicholas' Church in the High Street, which is seen here from the Culver Street side. The old church, which had been rebuilt as recently as 1875, was finally demolished in the mid-1950s and replaced with what is now called St Nicholas House. Part of the graveyard still survives and although perhaps not an inviting environment, still contains a number of memorial tombs and gravestones.

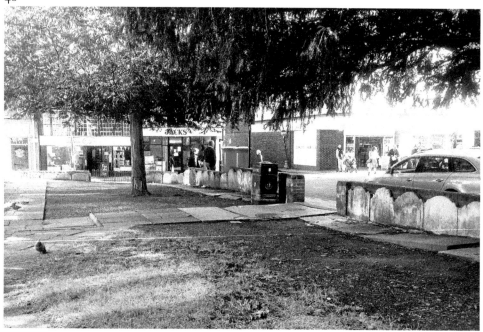

The graveyard as it appears today, showing several tombstones lined up against the wall.

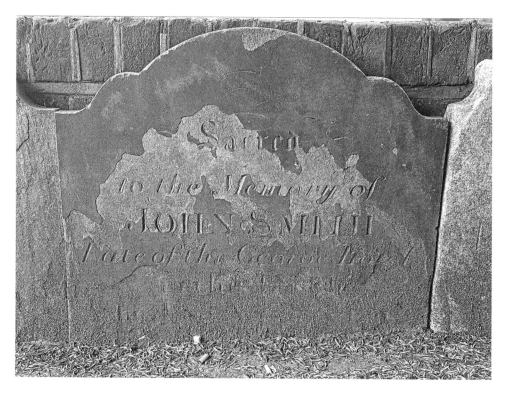

A close-up view of one of the tombstones. It is dedicated to John Smith of the George Hotel, who died on 27 November 1849, aged sixty-four.

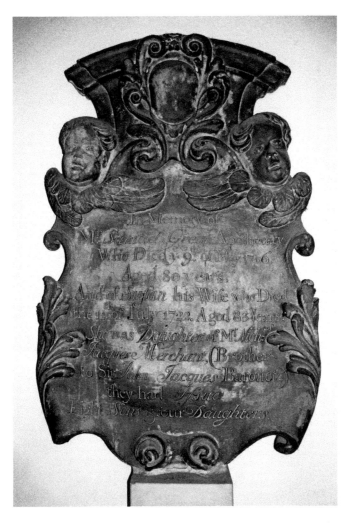

One of the memorials that was displayed inside St Nicholas' Church before its demolition in 1955 was this memorial tablet dedicated to Samuel Great, apothecary, who died on 9 May 1706. It can now be found on the wall of All Saints' Church (currently Colchester Natural History Museum). Samuel Great descended from a Dutch immigrant named Samuel De Groot (they later changed their name), who settled in the town sometime around 1600. Samuel became an apprentice to Robert Buxton, who was skilled at preparing the candied roots of the sea holly plant (*Eryngium maritimum*) that flourished around the Essex coastal regions at that time. The sweetmeats produced were considered a delicacy, having medicinal and aphrodisiac qualities and were known locally as Eringo roots. The recipe, which was a closely guarded secret, was eventually passed on to Samuel after Robert's death around 1665.

Samuel continued to trade from his former master's premises in the High Street, which was named 'The Old Twisted Posts and Pots' and located close to the Red Lion Inn. At some stage the family also owned the Red Lion and even today in the Red Lion yard one can still see a rainwater hopper, emblazoned with a red lion and the initials 'T.G.' for Thomas Great (son of Samuel). The business eventually passed to Samuel's descendants, who continued with the family speciality of making the candied Eringo until the death of Charles Great (Samuel's great-grandson) in 1797. The recipe was then passed on to a Mrs Thorn, who continued with its production until the late 1850s, after which production of the roots finally came to an end.

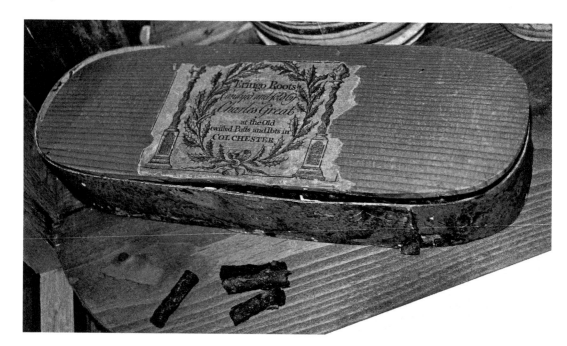

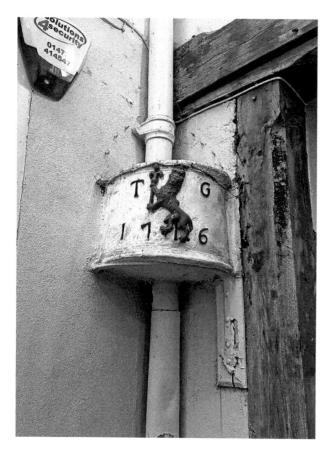

Above: This surviving box of Eringo roots, containing the name of Charles Great on its label, is part of the collection of the Colchester Museums Service after being presented to them by a local resident in 1931. Around the inscription on the lid there is a foliage wreath representing the sea holly, from which the Eringo was made and which, in turn, is flanked by a pair of twisted pillars standing on pedestals.

Left: The rainwater hopper in the Red Lion yard showing the initials of Thomas Great and dated 1716.

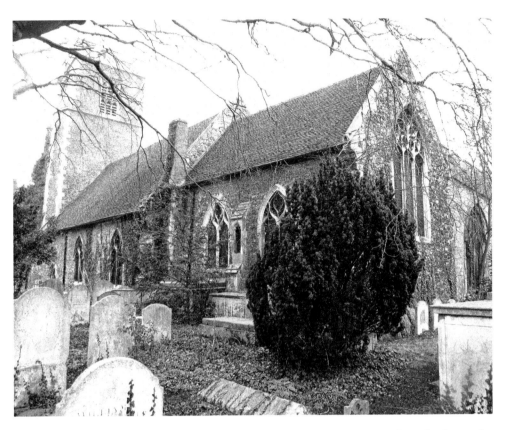

All Saints Church – now home to Colchester Natural History Museum. Apart from displaying the wall tablet dedicated to the memory of Samuel Great, there are numerous other memorials in the churchyard in remembrance of some of the town's past citizens.

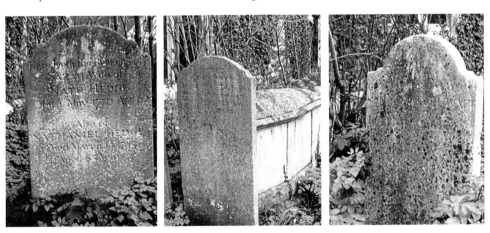

The stones depicted here mark the final resting places of some of Colchester's famous clockmakers including Nathaniel and Thomas Hedge and John Smorthwaite. John Smorthwaite, who traded from premises directly opposite the church in the High Street, is still remembered by a wall plaque on the building currently known as WH Shephard, Funeral Directors.

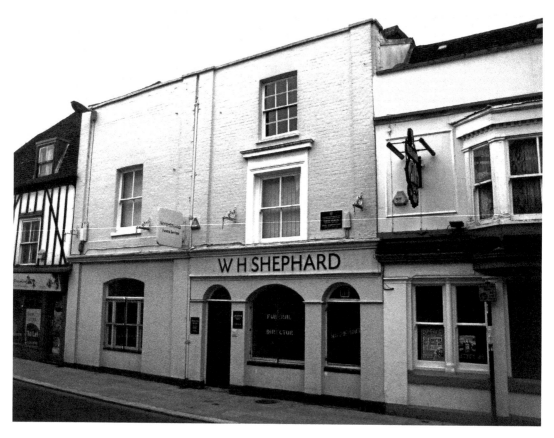

A wall plaque, seen above the shopfront of WH Shephard, shows the names of two former Colchester clockmakers, Jeremy Spurgin (1666–99) and John Smorthwaite (1675–1739), who both traded from this location.

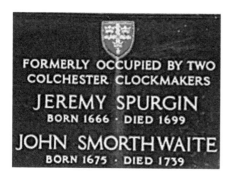

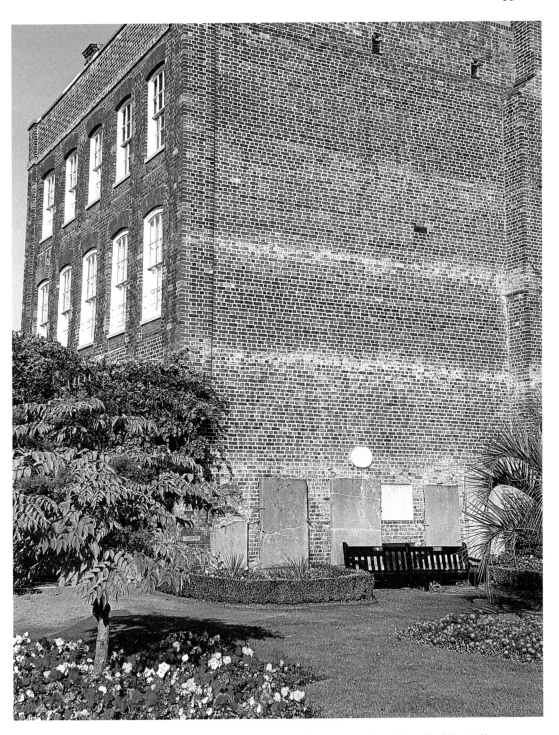

You may have noticed a number of gravestones standing against the side wall of the Hollytrees Museum when walking in the garden next to the building. These are mostly tombstones of the Honeywood family that were relocated to Colchester from St Margaret's Church at Markshall following its demolition in 1933.

THE FOUR STONES HERE SHOWN WERE REMOVED TO
COLCHESTER FROM MARKSHALL CHURCH ON ITS
DEMOLITION MARCH 1933.

(1) ROBERT HONYWOOD (1545-1627)
ELDEST OF THE 367 CHILDREN OF MARY HONYWOOD
WHOM SHE HAD AT HER DECEASE IN 1620 DESCENDED
FROM HER. HE BOUGHT MARKSHALL IN 1604.

(2) SIR THOS. HONYWOOD (1586-1666)
HIS SON, PARLIAMENTARIAN COMMANDER AT SIEGE
OF COLCHESTER 1648. M.P. FOR ESSEX. MEMBER OF
CROMWELL'S UPPER HOUSE 1657.

(3) DAME HESTER HONYWOOD (1607-1681)

(4) THOMAS HONYWOOD
THEIR ELDEST SON. OB. S.P. 1672

This stone is inscribed with the names of Robert Honeywood (1545–1627), the eldest of the 367 children that were descended from Mary Honeywood at the time of her death in 1620, and also to his son Sir Thomas Honeywood (1586–1666), Parliamentarian commander at the Siege of Colchester in 1648.

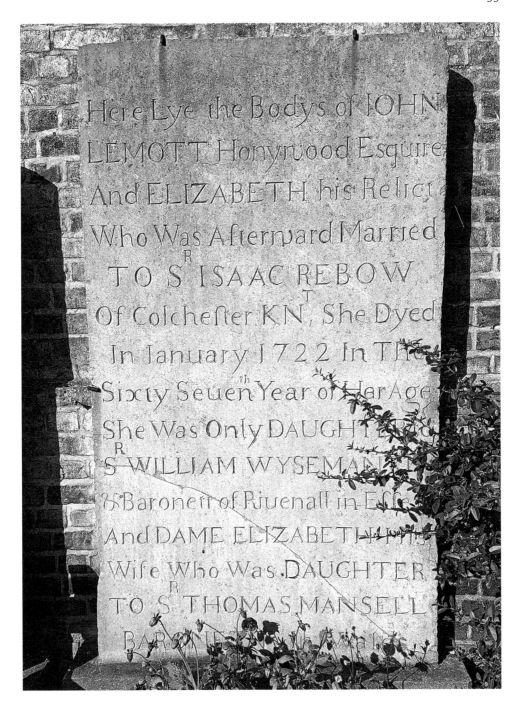

Here Lye the Bodys of IOHN LEMOTT Honywood Esquire And ELIZABETH his Relict Who Was Afterward Married TO S[R] ISAAC REBOW Of Colchefter KN[T], She Dyed In Ianuary 1722 In The Sixty Seuen[th] Year of Her Age She Was Only DAUGHTER to S[R] WILLIAM WYSEMAN &Baronett of Riuenall in Effex And DAME ELIZABETH His Wife Who Was DAUGHTER TO S[R] THOMAS MANSELL BARONETT ...

This stone records the name of John Lemotte Honeywood, son of Thomas Honeywood who figured in the Siege of Colchester. After he died in tragic circumstances in 1694 his widow Elizabeth (daughter of Sir William Wyseman, Baronet of Rivenhall) married Sir Isaac Rebow of Colchester. Sir Isaac is known to have entertained William III at his Head Street home on a number of occasions while the king was travelling to Harwich en route to the Continent. On one of these visits, on 27 March 1693, he was knighted by the king.

6. Buildings and Follies

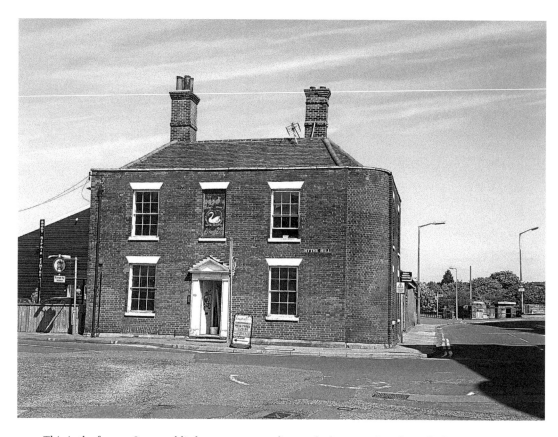

This is the former Swan public house, seen standing at the bottom of Hythe Hill. I'm sure that the building has a long and interesting history, but one particular event that took place in the early years of the nineteenth century is remembered in the form of some interesting graffiti scrawled on the brickwork to the right side of the door. This relates to the infamous 'Red Barn Murder', which took place at Polstead, Suffolk in 1827. William Corder, son of the local squire, had become involved with Maria Martin, the daughter of a poor family in the village. Having first promised to marry Maria he changed his mind and instead murdered her in the Red Barn and buried her body beneath the floor. Sometime later, after becoming concerned about her daughter's whereabouts, her mother had a strange dream in which her daughter had been murdered and buried beneath the floor of the barn.

After Maria's body was discovered a warrant was issued for the arrest of William Corder who was finally apprehended at Ealing in London – just one day before he had planned to escape to France. He was subsequently charged with Maria's murder at Whitechapel on 22 April 1828 and ordered to be returned to Suffolk to stand trial. He was thus put on the *Defiance* coach bound for Colchester in the custody of London policeman PC Lea. The local press took up the story and described the coach's arrival in the town: 'As the coach approached Colchester Corder recognised many persons but they didn't return his greetings. He was jeered as he passed by and the crowd followed him until he arrived at the George Hotel, where he retreated into a private room.'

Constable Lea then proceeded to Mr Smith, the governor of the Castle, which at this time was the county gaol, and asked him to receive the prisoner into his custody for the night. But Smith refused saying, 'I cannot take charge of him for I have nobody to look after him, and being charged with so dreadful an offence, it may be that he will lay violent hands upon himself for which I cannot be held accountable.' Eventually, it was decided that he should remain in the George and after eating a 'hearty supper' he retired to his room where he spent the night with one hand tied to the bedpost and the other to that of Constable Lea while he slept.

In the morning, after eating some light refreshment, Corder continued his journey to Polstead to attend the coroner's inquest, after which he was conveyed to Bury St Edmunds where he later stood trial for the murder of Maria Martin on 7 August 1728. After being found guilty he was hanged at Bury Gaol on Monday 11 August 1828. Back in Colchester one of the local residents – perhaps one of the customers of the Swan public house – recorded the event for posterity on the building's brickwork.

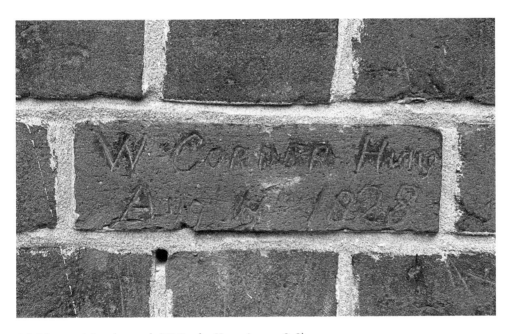

A brick containing the words 'W. Corder Hung Aug 11 1828'.

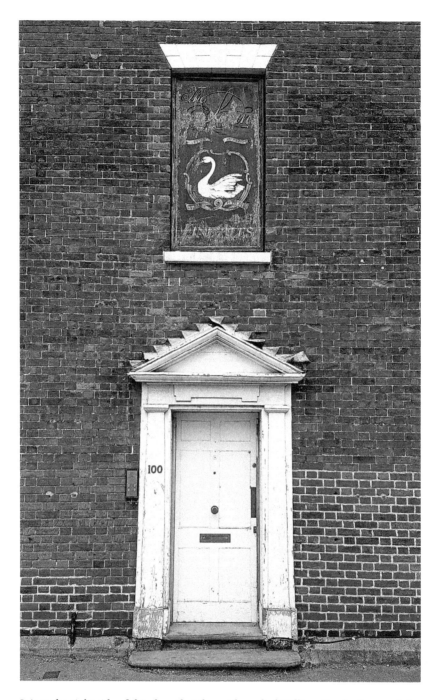

It is to the right side of this door that the grisly end of William Corder is recorded.

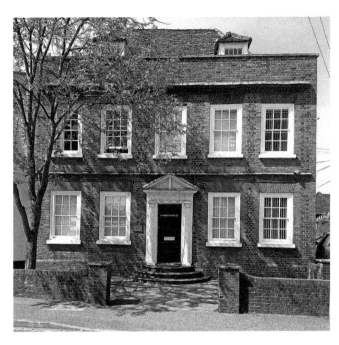

The old Custom House, seen here on Hythe Quay and dating from the early eighteenth century, stands very much as a lonely sentinel from a bygone age. In fact, very little of this once thriving port, which served the town for 800 odd years before its closure in 2001, survives to the modern day. In 1724, Daniel Defoe, the famous author and travel writer, was so impressed by the buzzing activity that he saw here during a visit to the town that he described the scene as 'The Wapping of Colchester'. He would no doubt have seen this building and perhaps even paid a visit. The building itself is thought to date from around 1720, but was almost certainly rebuilt over a previous structure based on the survival on some early sixteenth-century beams in the cellar. Even as late as the 1970s the Hythe was still considered to be one of the largest grain ports in the country and ships from Scandinavia, Holland, Germany and elsewhere were regular visitors to the port. However, within just a decade or so after this the port began to enter into a period of rapid decline before finally closing just a few years ago.

If the stones and walls of this building could speak they would surely have many a tale to tell, especially from the heyday of the smuggling trade in the eighteenth century. What had previously been considered as nothing more than a small-scale evasion of revenue duty had escalated into an industry of astonishing proportions. Smuggling was rife around the coastal areas of this country, and Essex was no exception. Almost every commodity was considered fair game to the smugglers who sought to avoid the revenue men at all costs. At one stage it was thought that as much as 75 per cent of all the tea drunk in England had escaped paying duty.

As far as the Colchester Customs House is concerned, the following case is typical of what the revenue men had to deal with. On Saturday 16 April 1748, at around 2 a.m., the peace and quiet of the area was disturbed by a large gang of horsemen – all fully armed with blunderbusses and pistols. Their aim was to break into the Customs House and help themselves to the store of illegal contraband that had previously been seized from smugglers plying the local rivers and ports.

According to a report related in the *Gentleman's Magazine* of the day, they proceeded to force open the King's warehouse with a large blacksmith's hammer and crow and succeeded in carrying off a large quantity of tea in sixty oil bags, weighing 1,514 pounds (nearly three-quarters of a ton!), which had previously been seized near Woodbridge by Captain Robert Martin of the Revenue cutter. The gang was eventually rounded up and convicted at Chelmsford Assizes in March 1752. Although up to fourteen people were known to have been involved in the crime, it was left to one unlucky individual named Samuel to take the blame and receive the death sentence for his part in the robbery.

but the petitioners were acquainted; that the late order was not intended to prejudice the freemen, but only to prevent unlawful combinations to distress the sufferers.

SATURDAY 9.

36 pieces of cannon, with their carriages, were shipt off for the Isle of *Sky* in *Scotland,* where two castles are erected for defence of that island against any future invasion or rebellion.

WEDNESDAY 13.

Sir *Peter Warren,* in the *Invincible,* with the *Chichester, Prince Frederick, Devonshire, Culloden,* and 4 *Dutch* men of war, sailed from St *Helen's* on a cruize.

SATURDAY 16.

Thirty smugglers with blunderbusses and pistols, at 2 in the morning, broke open the king's warehouse at *Colchester,* with a large blacksmith's hammer and crow, and carry'd off 60 oil bags, containing about 1514 pound of tea.

SUNDAY 17.

Came advice over land, that the *Anson,* Capt. *Fowles,* was taken in sight of *Bombay,* by the *Apollo* and *Anglesea,* 2 *French* men of war, after two hours resistance; but the captain had before sent 10 chests of treasure, and the company's dispatches on shore.———Admiral *Griffin* sailed from fort St *David, Sept.* 22, and next day burnt the *Neptune,* a *French* man of war, in *Madrass* road, and 'twas reported the *Princess Amelia,* formerly taken by the *French,* shared the same fate.———The cargo of the *Heathcote,* Capt. *Cape,* lost some weeks before, was seized by the *Moors,* who return'd one half.———The *French* ships, *Centaur,* 70 guns, *St Louis* and *Mars,* each 40, and the *Brilliant* 20, winter'd and refitted at *Goa,* whence they return'd to *Mibie, Oct.* 14, having lost many men by the *Goa* fever, and sailed from *Mibie, Oct.* 20, to cruise off the *Laccadiva* and *Maldiva* islands.——The *Princess Mary,* taken at *Madrass* was lost at *Goa,* in *July.*

MONDAY 18.

Eight men out of each company of

majesty for his execution.——Capt. *Laverick* and Mr *Priswick,* his second, were try'd for the murder of Capt. *Dawson* the 13th instant in a duel; the captain was found guilty of manslaughter, and *Priswick* acquitted.——*Levi* the *Jew,* for robbing the synagogue of *Aaron's* bells, &c. and *John Walker,* for stealing the coffin, shroud and body of *Francis Hill* lately executed, and selling it to a surgeon for a guinea, were order'd to be transported.

SUNDAY 24.

Mr *Thompson,* one of his majesty's messengers, arrived at the D. of *Newcastle's* office, with the instrument of preliminary articles for a general pacification, sign'd at *Aix la Chapelle,* by the ministers plenipotentiary of the K. of *Great Britain,* the most Christian King, and the States General. *Gaz.*

See the rise of stocks page 191.

TUESDAY 26.

A grant has passed the great seal to *Siphorus Paul* of *Woodchester, Gloucestershire,* clothier, for his new invented method of preparing cloth to be dy'd scarlet, so as more effectually to ground the colours, and preserve the beauty.

Another grant has passed to *Daniel Bridges* of *Hull,* apothecary for the sole use and benefit of his new-invented method of purifying rape-oil.

Roger Perkins has also obtained a grant of his new invention for making a spirit equal to *French* brandy from *British* materials.

On closing the poll for *Northamptonshire,* the numbers were, for *Valentine Knightley,* Esq; 2228, for *Wm Hanbury,* Esq; 2082; upon this a scrutiny was demanded for Mr *Hanbury,* but afterwards given up.

His majesty has given 1000 *l.* to the sufferers by fire in *Cornhill;* the Princesses *Amelia* and *Carolina* 100 *l.* the Lady *Betty Germain,* 50 *l.* the skinners and goldsmith's company each 50 *l.* above 300 *l.* produced by a play at *Covent Garden* theatre on the 6th.

IRELAND.

This page from the *Gentleman's Magazine* shows the case reported under the entry for Saturday 16 April 1748.

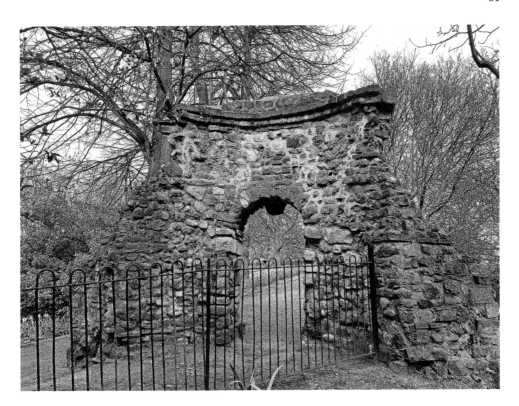

Above: This ornamental stone feature
can be seen just a few yards to the
right of the castle and at the start of
the terrace walk, which runs along
the top of the Norman bank before
terminating at a small classical-style
summerhouse at its western end.
The structure was created in 1747 by
Charles Gray (owner of Hollytrees
House) in the form of a rotunda
designed by James Deane, although
now only the entrance section
remains.

Right: Detail from a town plan in
Philip Morant's *History of Colchester*
(1748), showing Gray's terrace
running on top of the old Norman
bank between the rotunda at one end
and the summerhouse at the other.

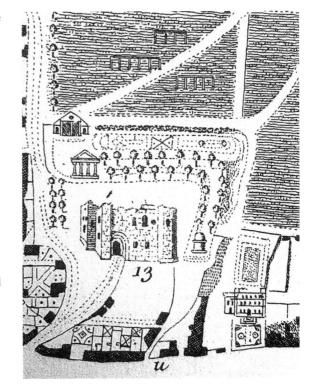

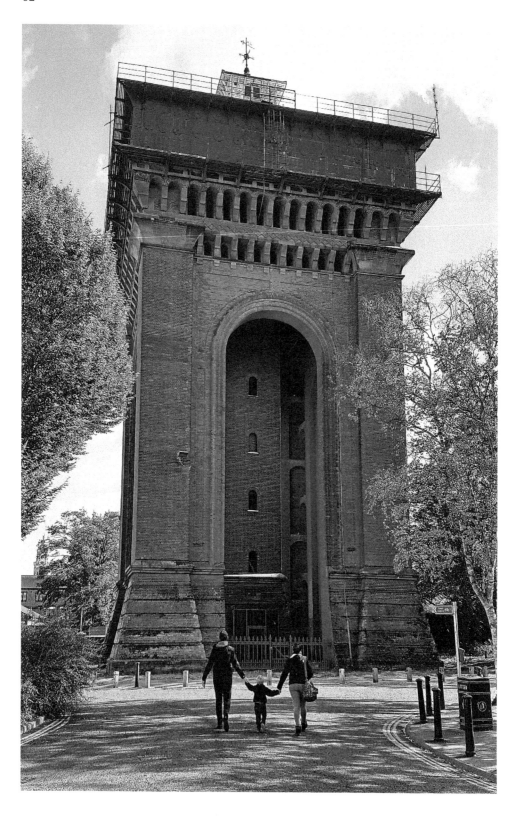

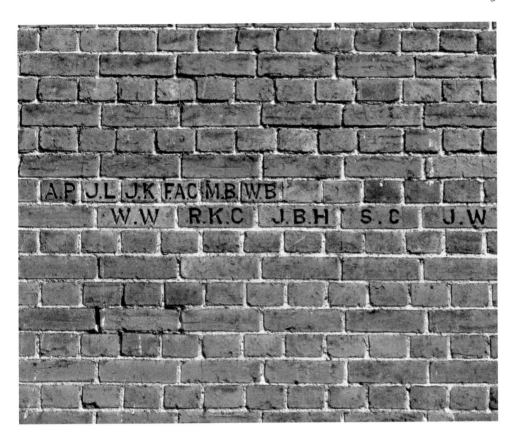

Above: Here are some of the 'Corporation Bricks' containing the initials of several prominent figures of the day, including John Bawtree Harvey, John Kent (from Kent Blaxill) and James Wicks.

Opposite: One of the more iconic features to be seen on the town's historic skyline is 'Jumbo', the Victorian water tower, which was built in 1882 to provide the people of Colchester – or at least those who lived in the town centre – with a steady supply of piped water. How many times, however, have you been right up close to the tower – a hundred times, a thousand times? Whatever the answer, have you ever noticed the 'Corporation Bricks'? If you look carefully around 30 feet up from the ground on the right-hand leg of the tower, when standing with the Roman wall behind you, you will see fifteen bricks each with two or three letters engraved on them.

To understand just why these bricks were laid here in the first place we need to go back to the summer of 1882 when Councillor James Wicks, who headed the Water Works Committee, decided that he would like to organise a little ceremony at which he would lay an official foundation stone at the base of the new water tower. However, not everyone on the Committee was in agreement with his suggestion and the event failed to materialise, and 'Jumbo' began to rise from its foundations. However Wicks, being a resourceful man, was not to be outdone and just a few months later, in October 1882, Wicks finally got his way – well, almost. By this time the tower was around 30 feet off the ground and a number of local councillors, including the town's two Members of Parliament, were invited to ascend a tall ladder to a special platform to lay a commemoration brick emblazoned with their own initials to mark this special occasion. After the ceremony the group were entertained to a champagne reception funded by Wicks himself, who also gave half a crown (25p) to each of Everett's workmen. As it turned out, only eleven of the twenty-four committee members bothered to attend. Those who did attend were joined by James Wicks himself, Mr Everett, the builder, and the two local Members of Parliament.

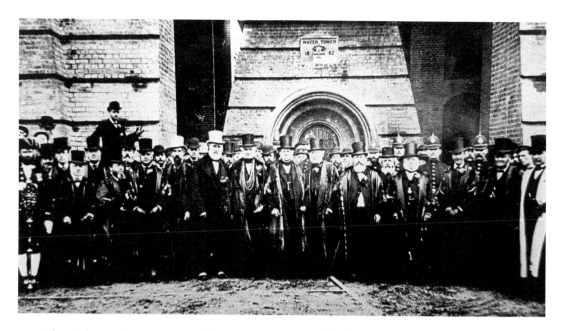

Above: The opening ceremony of the new water tower took place on 27 September 1883 and was attended by most members of the council and other interested parties. In the centre of the picture, wearing the mayoral chain, is John Bawtree Harvey (see the bricks) and the second gentleman seen on his right, wearing a white top hat, is James Wicks himself.

Opposite above: At first glance this interesting small brick and stone structure located just outside the entrance to Firstsite seems perhaps to have had medieval origins. However, when viewed from the opposite direction inside the Minories garden a much different aspect presents itself. In fact, what is seen is a typical eighteenth-century Gothic-style summerhouse, possibly modelled on a design by the famous garden designer of the period Batty Langley (1696–1751). In earlier times the building was included in the garden of neighbouring East Hill House, before being sold off with part of the garden to the owners of the Minories in 1923. In its original setting the summerhouse was designed to provide a resting place at the end of a garden walk or terrace. In fact, the remaining part of this former terrace still survives running behind East Hill House, although today it is mainly used for car parking.

Opposite below: The summerhouse as seen from the Minories garden.

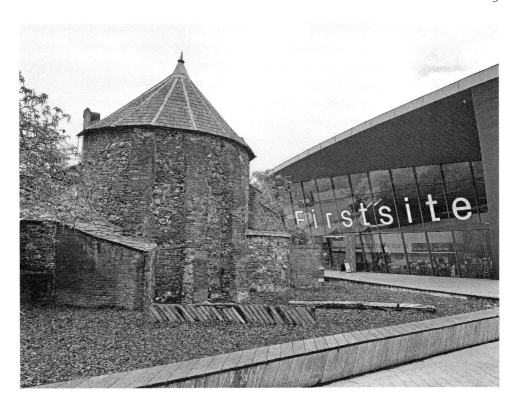

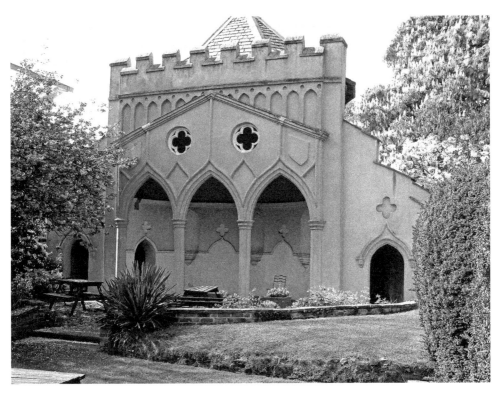

Opposite above: This picturesque view of Bourne Mill and pond can hardly be described as a 'secret' in any sense of the word, but it is somewhat off the beaten track and remains unvisited by many people. However, it certainly has a lot going for it and is currently the only building in Colchester that is owned by the National Trust.

The mill and pond were originally owned by the monks of St John's Abbey before coming into the hands of the Lucas family in 1590, who had themselves already taken possession of the abbey site in 1548 following the Dissolution of the Monasteries in the late 1530s. Whatever type of building stood on the site prior to this period, in 1591 Sir Thomas Lucas set about rebuilding the mill as a private fishing lodge, presumably using much material recycled from the ruins of the abbey. In later years, however, it reverted to being a fulling mill in the cloth trade and also a flour mill.

Architecturally, the building is of much interest, incorporating large amounts of medieval stone and Roman brick as well its distinctive Dutch gable ends, which were so popular at the time. As noted above, the mill became associated with the local cloth industry and many of the processes involved in the trade, such as fulling, were carried out at the mill. When the cloth trade finally ceased to operate locally in the 1830s the building later reverted to a flour mill until its final closure in 1935. In the late nineteenth century a number of interviews with former cloth workers who once worked at the mill were carried out by Dr Henry Laver, so we do have something of an insight into what working conditions would have been like there in the early 1800s.

One of the interviews that Dr Laver conducted was with seventy-five-year-old Charles Baker while he was a resident in the workhouse in the late 1890s. Among other things, he had much to say about his time working at the mill in the last days of the bay-making industry in the late 1820s and early 1830s:

I was born in Colchester in 1817 and when I was nine years old in 1826 I went to work at Bourne Pond Mill, which was then owned by Mr Peter Devall, a master baymaker, who lived in Priory Street just below St James' Church. At the mill I helped with a number of the various processes, including the fulling of the cloth. This was the final process associated with the trade and it was carried on like this. We folded a piece of bay on the floor, so that it made a pile about a yard square, and as we did so we sprinkled it with chamber lye (urine). We used to go round to the workhouses and other places to collect the chamber lye for which we paid a ha'penny a pail. By the following morning the bays had heated. We then took these and put them two of three pieces at a time under the fulling stocks – large wooden beams which rubbed them in a certain way, thus fulling or thickening them. This rubbing process continued for about half an hour, after which a good stream of water was turned on to the bays to wash them. We used to make the water very foul in fulling; I have seen the Distillery Pond quite white after we had done.

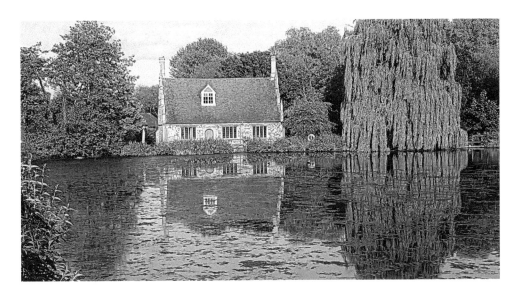

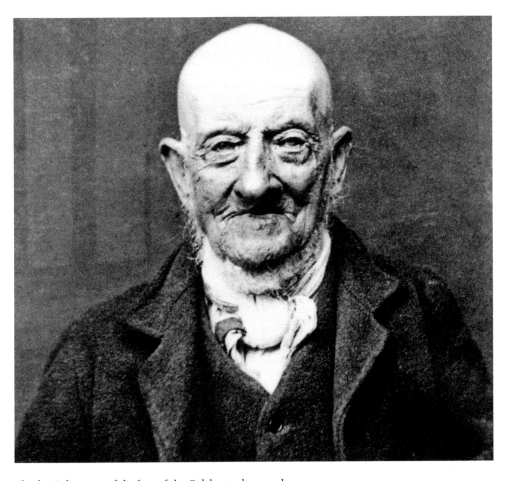

Charles Baker, one of the last of the Colchester bay-workers.

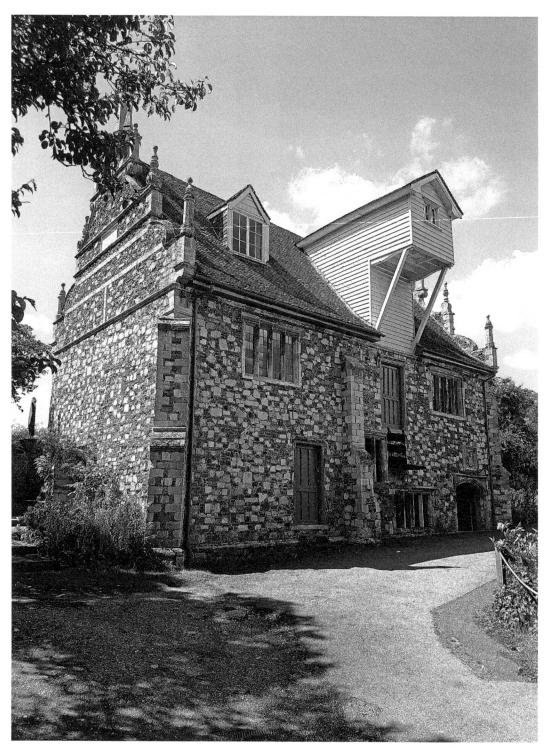

This view of the mill is seen from the opposite direction from the pond and shows the lower level side of the building, which also contains the wheelhouse.

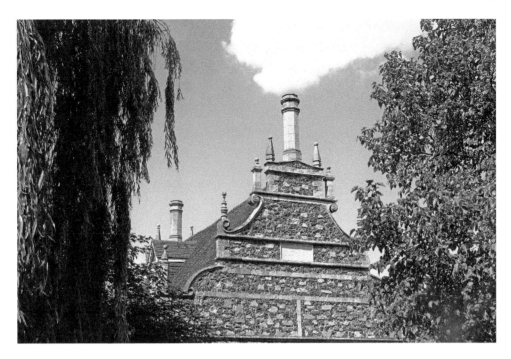

One of the building's interesting architectural features are its ornate Dutch-style gable ends, a feature that was fashionable in the Lowland countries of Europe at this time.

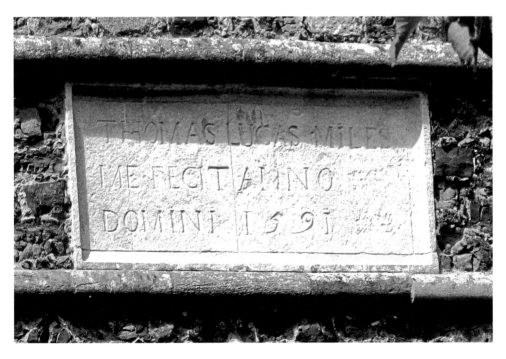

This stone panel on one of the gable ends tells us that the mill was built by Sir Thomas Lucas in 1591 ('Thomas Lucas Miles Me Fecit Anno Domini 1591').

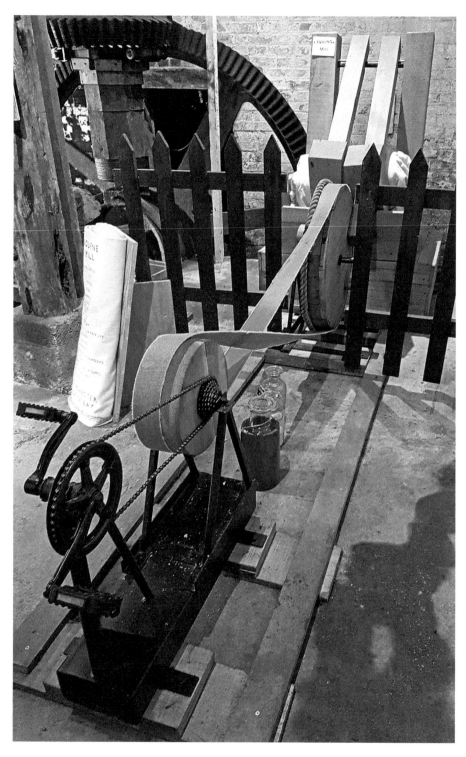

A recent addition to the mill has been the installation of a scaled-down set of fulling stocks, which are operated by pedal power rather than by water.

7. Almshouses for the Poor

One of Colchester's collective legacies from its relatively more recent past (the sixteenth century onwards) has been the provision of a number of charitable foundations in the form of almshouses for the poor. Originally known as hospitals, these foundations provided free accommodation and a small weekly allowance to those in advancing years who had fallen upon hard times. Although the concept of free accommodation and a weekly allowance has since passed by the wayside, these homes still provide much needed accommodation for many residents of the town.

By far the largest of these foundations is that which was originally provided under the terms of the will of Arthur Winsley, a baymaker and former mayor and alderman of the town. In his will, which was proved in 1727, he left £500 for the Brick House farm building, located in the Old Heath area of the town, to be converted into twelve convenient apartments for the habitation of twelve ancient men. He further stipulated that each of the apartments was to consist of a low room, a chamber, a garret and a garden to every dweller as near as may be in form to Mr John Winnock's charity houses now are.

He further decreed that each of the almsmen was to receive a weekly payment of 2s 6d (12½p), as well as a chaldron of coal to be delivered annually to each resident (note: a London chaldron equalled thirty-six bushels, which weighed around 25 hundredweights – 2,800 lbs/1,270 kg). It was further ordered that no women were to be admitted to partake of the said charity, nor any man under the age of sixty at the time of his admittance. In practice this meant that any widows remaining after their husband's death were obliged to move out and find other accommodation. The bequest also stipulated that no children were to be admitted to the almshouses. Additionally, the sum of 10s (50p) a year was to be paid to a good preacher, chosen by the trustees, to preach a sermon to the said poor men every New Year's Day along with a further 20s (£1) to provide the poor men with a festive dinner on the same day.

As time went on, the weekly allowance paid to each of the residents was increased – rising to 10s by 1879. However, this payment was finally discontinued in 1956 and the gift of coal was discontinued in 1958. As for the free annual dinner at New Year, this was replaced in 1873 with a payment of 3s (15p) to each of the residents – later changed to 25p in 1972. In addition to this, each resident was also treated to some free sweets on Christmas Day – a tradition that has only lapsed in recent years. Today each resident is still treated to a free festive meal once a year as well as the occasional free outing in the summer months. Over the years the charity has benefited from numerous other benefactors, resulting in more accommodation being slowly added. Today the trust is responsible for eighty apartments that house around 100 residents – both single and married couples.

Arthur Winsley's will also included a bequest of £250 to be used for a monumental statue of himself, which was to be erected in St James' Church. His will states,

> I give two hundred and fifty pounds to be laid out on a Monument to be erected against the south wall of the said church, with my statue cut out in marble, lying with the left hand under the head, and a book in the right hand, and in a night gown, with inscriptions as my most judicious friends shall think proper.

As it turned out, his 'most judicious friends' must have thought it somewhat improper for him to be depicted entirely in his nightclothes and instead had him portrayed a little more formally dressed, reclining in a long open coat or robe over a buttoned waistcoat and open-necked shirt. Although the monument is not signed, the work is believed to be by one Richard Van Spanger, who was possibly working to a design by the well-known architect James Gibbs and received a payment of £203 for the work in 1738. It seems highly likely that Mr Van Spanger was also responsible for completing the maquette (a scaled-down model) of the main statue, which can still be seen in the chapel at Winsley's Almshouses. The maquette is only around a fifth of the size of the final composition in St James' Church, and is of terracotta rather than marble.

Finally, it is of interest to note that although Winsley requested that his statue should be placed in St James' Church, he was not a practicing Anglican but a dedicated Nonconformist who attended the Independent Meeting House in Moor Lane (Priory Street), the congregation of which later moved to the new church in Lion Walk in 1766. In order for him to have held civic office, which he did by becoming mayor of the town in 1721, he would have been obliged to have been a partaker of Holy Communion in an Anglican church. And from the surviving records we can see that he duly complied with this requirement – on one occasion at least – in 1719.

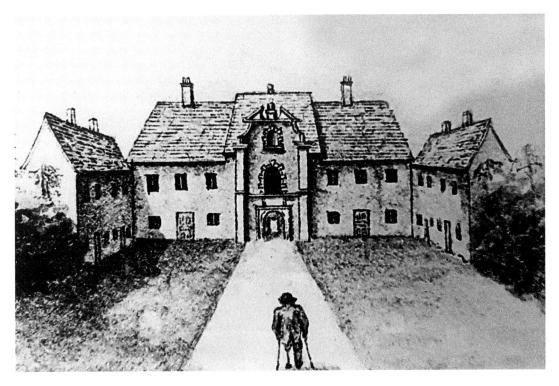

Winsley's almshouses as seen in 1801.

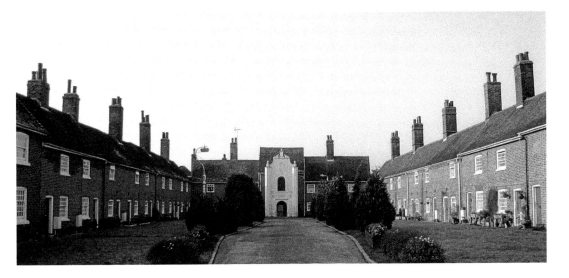

The same view in 2017.

291

A List of the Persons Appointed to receive the Donors Char[...]

Names.	Time of admission.	Names.	Time of admission.
W: Featherston.		Jn.º Reeve ... 29.th March 1744	
Wm Woodham		Sam.l Hocker ... 9.th April 1745	
Lyonel: Mudd		Jn.º Sadler ... 8.th May ... 1746	
Hen.y Spurham		Dan.l Mortier ... 25.th Feby. 1746	
Rob.t Wiles	Appointed 13: January 1734.	Tho.s Fitch ... 5.th April 1748	
Tho.s Garnett		Wm Sherman — 12.th Octob.r 1749	
Jn.º Verlander		Wm Freeman	
Wm Verlander		Jn.º Agnis 29.th March 174[.]	
Rob.t Eslen		Frn. Hawkins 27: April 174[.]	
Tho.s Smith		Jn.º Andrews ... 16.th Nov.r 174[.]	
Geo: Monk		Jn.º Laslen ... 3: Septemb.r 175[.]	
Cha.s Stebbing		Ja.s Cricket 20.th Decemb.r 175[.]	
		Sim.n Clay ... 18.th Decemb.r 175[.]	
		Jn.º Cutler ... 29 ... D.º 175[.]	
Jn.º Booler ... 19.th March 1735		Corn. Harrington 9.th Feby. 175[.]	
Isa: Everitt ... 6.th May ... 1736		Wm Dawes ... 9.th Jany. 175[.]	
Ben: Clamtree 1: January 1737		Rob.t Leech ... 2: April 175[.]	
Tho.s Burton 1.st ... D.º 1737		Rich. Wright 28.th Decem.r 175[.]	
Rich. Wright 26.th March 1742		Ja.s Gunn	
Jn.º Overstall		Jn.º Cook 8.th March 175[.]	
Ja.s Wilbee 1: June 1742		Tho.s Porter ... 1: Jany. 1759	
Hen.y Downes		Sam.l Smith ... 5.th June 175[.]	
James Bowler 28.th April 1743		Jn.º Chapman 12.th Aug.t 1759	
Tho.s Pain ... 8 Septemb.r 1743		Sam.l Steel ... 30.th Jany. 1760	
Ben: Welleum		Wm Freeman 9.th April 1760	
Sam.l Salmon 1. Feby. 1744		Peter Tayspil ... 1.st Dec.r 1760	
Edw. Coveney refused on acc.t of his [...]		Sam.l Shearcroft 16.th Jany. 1760	

This page from the trustee's minute book from 1734 shows the names of the initial twelve almsmen, followed by their subsequent replacements once they had either died or given up their accommodation.

WINSLEY'S ALMSHOUSES.

Extract from the Donor's Will, ARTHUR WINSLEY, an Alderman of the Borough of Colchester, the Founder of this Charity, who died on January 30th, 1726.

That no Profane Person given to Swearing, Drinking, or any other Vice be Admitted; and if any of them be found so Guilty, that they be turned out by the Major part of the Trustees. And if any one of the said Men be Contentious, and Disturb the Peace of the rest, or be Guilty of any Indecent Acts, they shall be liable to be discharged by the Trustees.

My Will is, that no Children be Admitted into the said Apartments.

It is further Ordered and Decreed, by the High Court of Chancery, that the Men, who are to partake of this Charity do observe the Restrictions in the said Will, relative to the Government of the said Charity; and that if any of them shall be Guilty of any Offence contrary thereto, the said Trustees, or the Major part of them, be at liberty to remove such Persons.

Above: This extract from Arthur Winsley's will still hangs on the walls of many of the resident's homes.

Right: This view shows the rear view of the chapel and ground-floor entrance leading out into the main square.

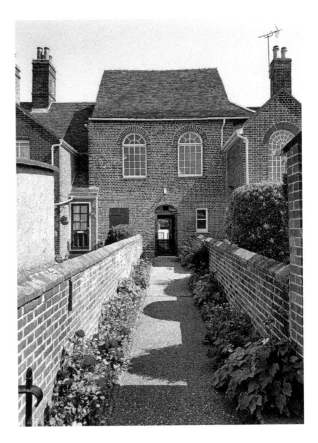

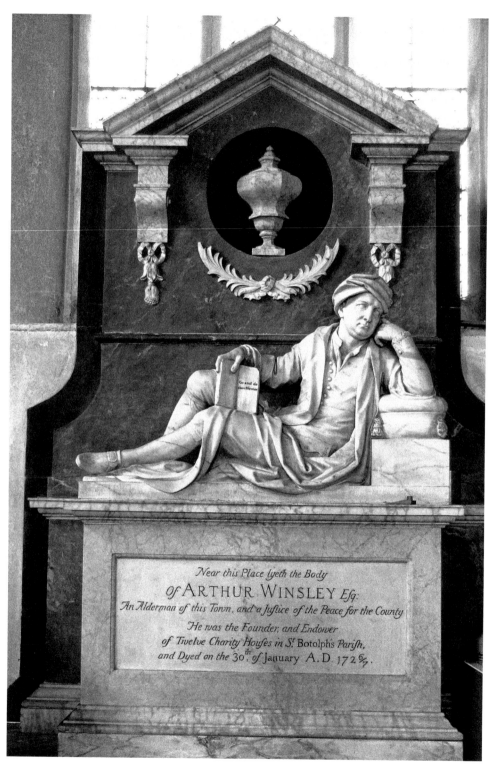

Near this Place lyeth the Body
of ARTHUR WINSLEY *Esq:*
An Alderman of this Town, and a Justice of the Peace for the County
He was the Founder, and Endower
of Twelve Charity Houses in S.t Botolph's Parish,
and Dyed on the 30.th of January A.D. 172 8/9.

Winsley's marble monument, which stands just inside St James' Church

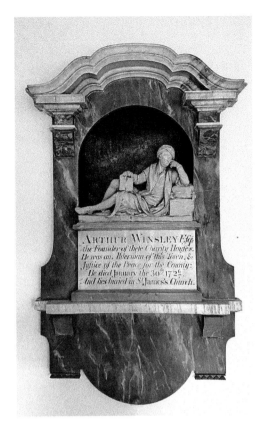

Right: This maquette, or working model, of the original version can be seen on the chapel wall at Winsley's almshouses. It is approximately one fifth of the size of the original version in St James' Church.

Below: This close-up view of Winsley's statue shows the difference in quality between the main marble model and the smaller terracotta version.

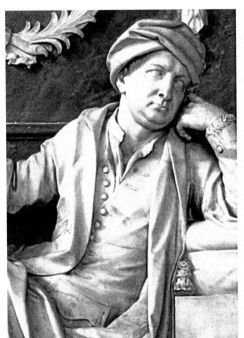

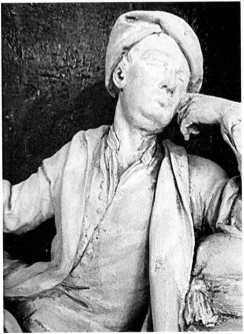

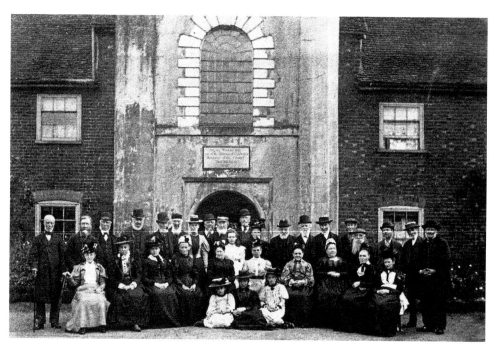

Here we see two contrasting views of the residents of the almshouses. The older picture was taken in 1898 and the modern version in 2017.

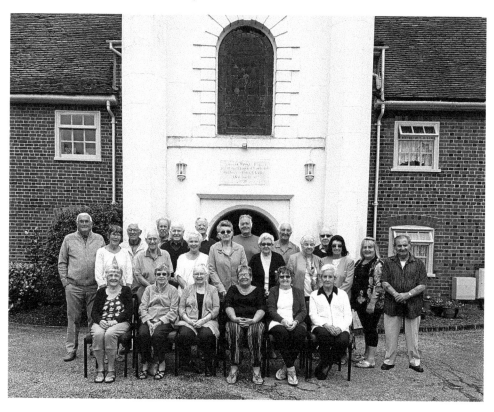

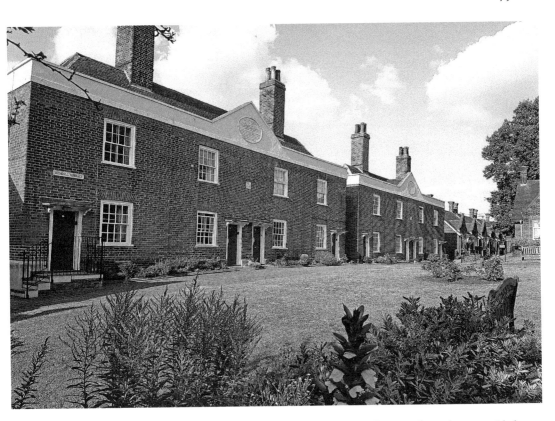

Another group of almshouses, located just off Military Road and not far away from those provided by Arthur Winsley, are those known as Kendall's Almshouses. They were erected in 1791 as a charitable gift from John and Ann Kendall, assisted by other subscribers. John and his wife were committed Quakers in the town and John was to spend several years of his life travelling around the country on related missionary work. The initial accommodation block that they provided, seen to the left here, was built to provide accommodation for eight poor widows upwards of the age of sixty, with priority given to those whose husbands had died in Arthur Winsley's charity houses and who had been required to move out. In a similar way to the benefit system of Winsley's charity, each resident was to receive 3s a week and a chaldron of coal every year. An additional building and almost identical to the first structure (seen on the right of the picture) was erected in 1806 for the accommodation of another eight poor women of the town.

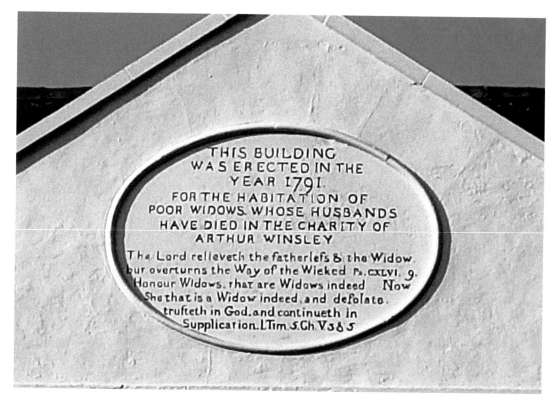

THIS BUILDING
WAS ERECTED IN THE
YEAR 1791.
FOR THE HABITATION OF
POOR WIDOWS WHOSE HUSBANDS
HAVE DIED IN THE CHARITY OF
ARTHUR WINSLEY
The Lord relieveth the fatherlefs & the Widow
bur overturns the Way of the Wicked Ps. CXLVI. 9.
Honour Widows. that are Widows indeed Now
She that is a Widow indeed, and defolate.
trufteth in God. and continueth in
Supplication. I Tim. 5. Ch V. 3 & 5

A wall plaque on the central pediment of Kendall's Almshouses showing details of the building's dedication in 1791.

Almost opposite Kendall's Almshouses in Military Road (which was then known as Hog Lane) is another row of buildings known as Winnock's Almshouses, which were built in 1678 by John Winnock, who was a member of the Dutch congregation and a wealthy baymaker. In fact, the original six dwellings were initially provided to benefit, 'the Poore of the Dutch Congregacion in Colchester', but over time the main beneficiaries of the charity tended to be aged women from the town. In a similar manner to the previous almshouses already mentioned, other buildings were later added to the main block, thereby providing further accommodation. In 1976 both Winnock's and Kendall's charities were amalgamated under one scheme, known as Winnock's and Kendall's Combined Almshouse Charity.

Architecturally speaking, the original block of six houses are perhaps the oldest domestic brick buildings in Colchester. The front aspect of the building is particularly attractive, containing a number of interesting brick features. The row is divided by the addition of a number of brick pilasters rising from ground-floor level and continuing through a deep moulded-brick string course before stopping just short of the parapet. The string course itself almost gives an impression of a classical-style entablature separating the two levels. In the central section, which is surmounted by a large plain pediment, we see a smaller but more ornate pediment lower down, set above the two central doors and including two stone panels containing the initials of John and Mary Winnock and the date '1678'.

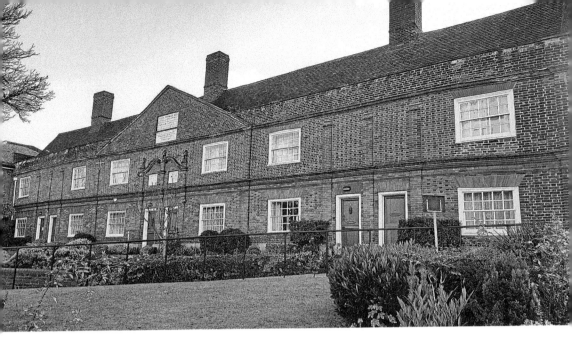

Winnock's Almshouses, erected in 1678.

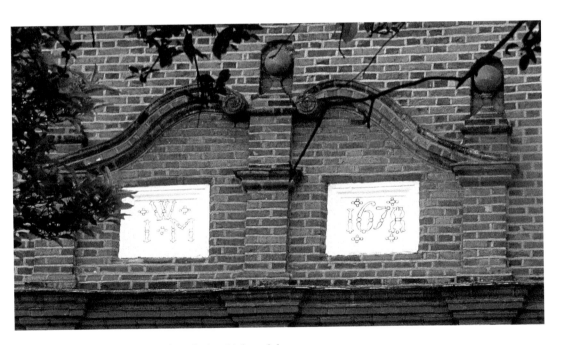

Stone panels showing the founder's initials and date.

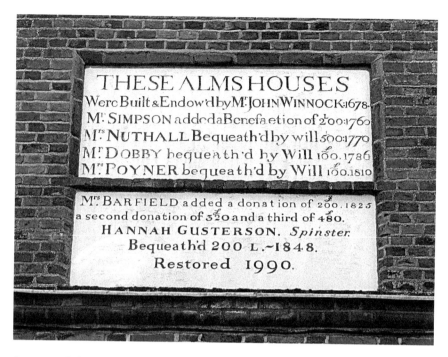

THESE ALMS HOUSES
Were Built & Endow'd by M: JOHN WINNOCK 1678.
M: SIMPSON added a Benefaction of 200.1760.
M: NUTHALL Bequeath'd by will 500.1770
M: DOBBY bequeath'd by Will 100.1786
M: POYNER bequeath'd by Will 100.1810

M: BARFIELD added a donation of 200.1825
a second donation of 320 and a third of 480.
HANNAH GUSTERSON. Spinster.
Bequeath'd 200 L.~1848.
Restored 1990.

Stone panel showing the names and bequests of subsequent benefactors to the charity.

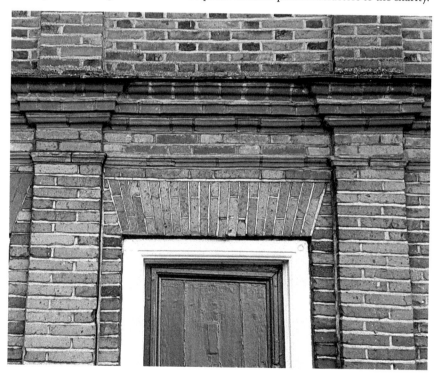

A close-up view of the moulded-brick string course running across the front of the almshouses.

8. Fountains, Monuments, Ruins and Other Structures

Something must have been going on in Colchester in the summer of 1864, for at least two new drinking fountains were unveiled to the public within just a few weeks of each other. The first, which can be seen in the adjacent view at the top of East Hill, concerned the opening of a fountain set within the wall of East Hill House. The unveiling of the fountain took place on Monday 1 August following an elaborate ceremony involving both the rector and churchwardens of St James' parish, as well as a large number of parishioners and the band of the Essex Rifles Regiment.

This was a time, of course, when improvements to public health were very much at the forefront in many people's minds and the installation of public drinking fountains was gaining momentum around the country. After several decades of battling with numerous outbreaks of cholera and other water-borne deceases, the provision of a clean supply of drinking water was at last being seen as a priority in many quarters. In Colchester, Mrs Margaret Round of East Hill House, well known for her humanitarian support for such causes, decided to do something about it.

The fountain, which was set into the boundary wall of her property, included the biblical words, 'With joy shall ye draw water' (Isaiah 12:3), which would no doubt have been a joy to many people who had just trudged their way up East Hill on a hot summer's day. At a lower level the words 'In Memoriam' were inscribed, which highlighted the fact that the fountain had been provided in memory of her later husband, George Round, who had died in 1857. Water would no doubt have been continuously issuing from the spout of the fountain and there would probably also have been a cup attached to a chain to drink from. Below the fountain was a stone step, which would have enabled children to have gained access, and set aside at a low level to the left was a separate trough for dogs to gain refreshment.

It is not known when the fountain fell into disuse, but it was certainly still in working order during the First World War as can be seen from the following comments by Alice Twyman (b. 1906), a local resident who lived nearby and who could recall seeing the fountain still being used at that time:

> I can remember seeing a line of soldiers marching up East Hill during the First World War, some of whom were fainting by the roadside, and when they got to the top of the hill they all broke ranks and had a drink of water from the tap, or fountain, in the wall.

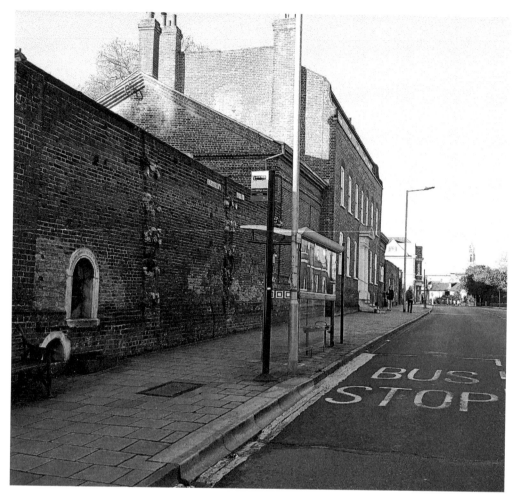

The drinking fountain set in the wall at the top of East Hill.

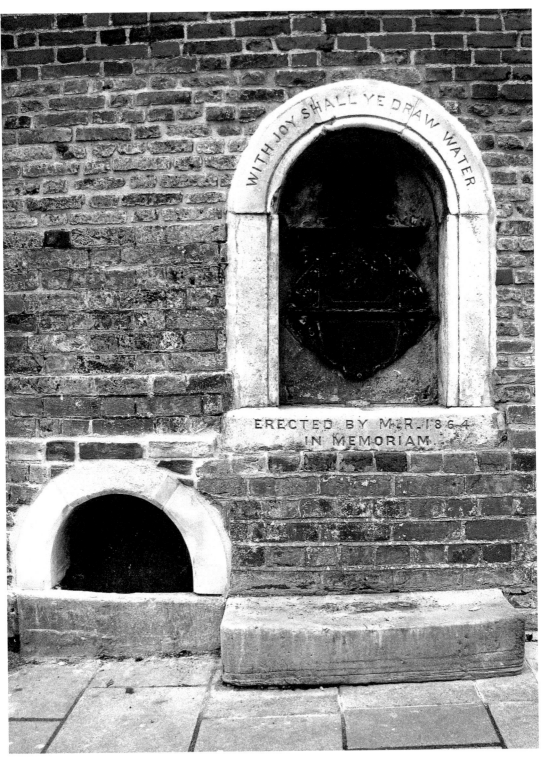

A close-up view of the former drinking fountain set in the wall of East Hill House.

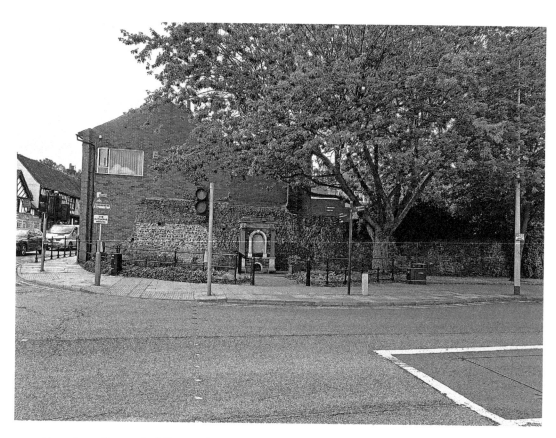

Above: Just a few weeks following the opening of the East Hill fountain a far more elaborate version was unveiled outside what was then the new cattle market at Middleborough. This event took place on Saturday 27 August 1864 and was very much a civic affair, being attended by the mayor of Colchester and several other members of the town council. As can be seen from the picture the fountain itself (which currently stands against the Roman wall near the bottom of North Hill) was a rather imposing structure, of classical appearance and built mainly of brick, stone and marble. The water supply itself came directly from the town's mains and would have flowed from a porcelain shell into a circular marble basin, and from there to a smaller basin at ground level providing water for dogs. The design also allowed for the overflow from the fountain to then be directed to augment the water supply for the cattle in the market, which was supplied from a well. Finally, an ornamental double bronze gas lamp was fitted to the top of the fountain.

The fountain was the gift of Taverner John Miller, a wealthy businessman who ran a whaling and shipping business based in London and who had decided to enter the realm of politics a few years earlier. He was first elected MP for Maldon in the 1852 general election, but following an investigation into corrupt practices (in which he was cleared of complicity) the election was declared void, leading to a by-election the following year. Miller later stood, unsuccessfully, as MP for Colchester in 1857 but won the seat in the general election the following month and continued to serve as the town's MP until his resignation in February 1867.

Opposite above: A close-up view of the fountain.

Opposite below: This early view looking up North Hill from Middleborough around 1900 shows the drinking fountain in its original position outside the cattle market. When the market finally closed in the 1970s, the fountain was removed to its present position next to the Roman wall.

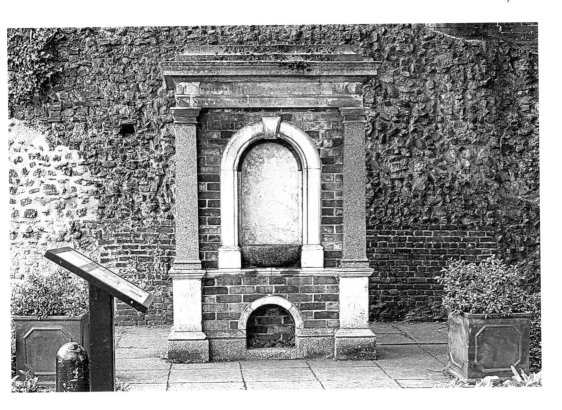

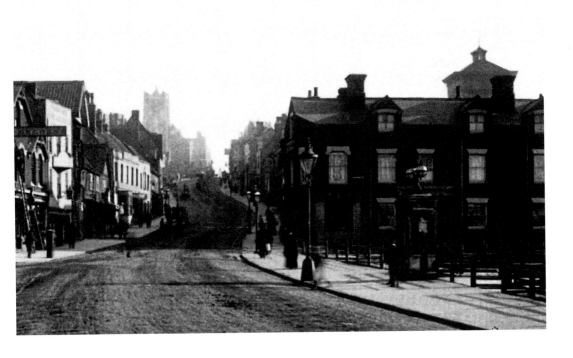

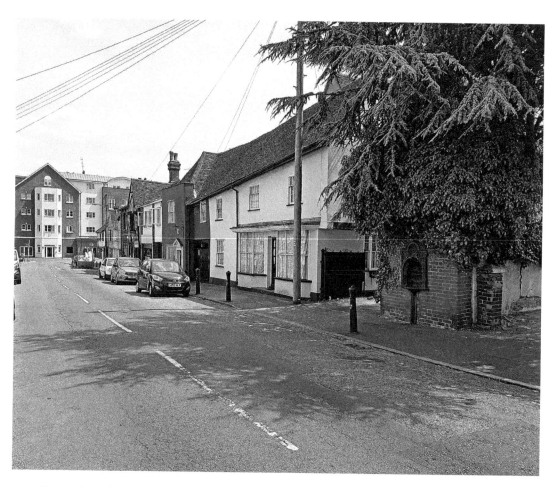

Here we have the remains of yet another drinking fountain, located by the roadside at the bottom of Hythe Hill. The fountain was installed in 1899, with the cost of the installation being met by Alderman James Paxman. The fountain was manufactured at the Saracen foundry in Glasgow by Macfarlane Ltd, one of the main suppliers of such fountains at the time. The design chosen was taken from their published catalogue (design No. 17) and includes an image of a ship (an optional extra) set within a circular shield above the main arch. This was probably to highlight the importance of the harbour area of the town and the many Thames sailing barges that regularly visited the port. Although the Hythe area had a mains water supply at this time, in many cases this only extended to outside water closets and perhaps a single cold tap in the kitchen. Many of the poorer families still relied on standpipes and pumps in the street for their drinking water. In fact, it was only when the drinking fountain mentioned above was installed that the old roadside pump in the same location was done away with.

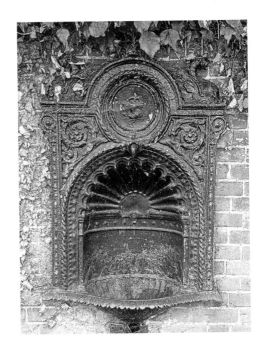

Right: A close-up view of the fountain showing the decorated arch and the image of a ship in the shield above. Originally there would have been a tap fixed above the basin as well as a cup attached to a chain to drink from.

Below: This is part of a page from William Macfarlane's catalogue (*c.* 1885) showing fountain design No. 17 in the bottom left corner. According to the firm's price list this fountain would have cost £5 6s 9d (£5.34), which in today's money would be over £4,000 based on average earnings.

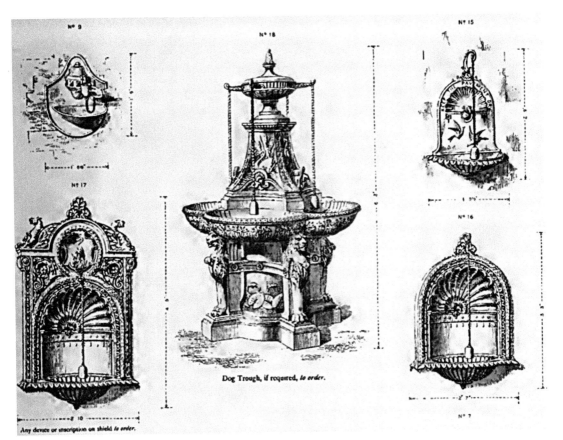

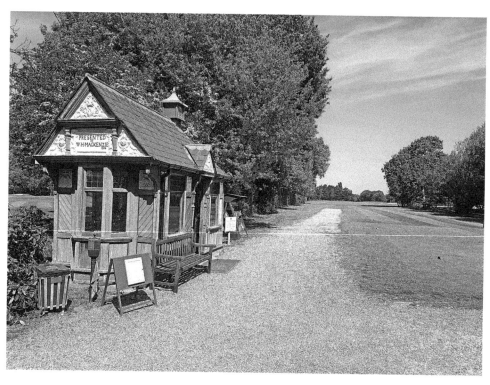

This interesting-looking building currently standing next to the 11th tee at the Colchester Golf Club at Braiswick has an interesting history. Although the structure has been an integral part of the golf club since its formation back in 1907, the building itself once stood in the middle of Colchester High Street. The inscription seen on the gable end of the building shows that the structure was presented by W. H. Mackenzie (William Henderson Mackenzie) in 1894 – not to the golf club of the town, but rather as a shelter for the town's horse cabbies.

Mr Mackenzie, a town councillor, provided the building at his own expense to be used by the town's horse-cab drivers who operated from the nearby cab rank in the High Street. In a letter sent to the town council in January 1894, he says the following,

> Dear Sir, for some time past I have been struck with the insufficient accommodation provided for the Colchester cabmen to protect them from the inclemency of the weather, and am now writing to inform you that I have had a shelter of an ornamental and useful kind built of old English oak, and well-seasoned, which I wish to present to the Corporation for the sole use of the Colchester cabmen.

Councillor Mackenzie's generous gift was accepted by the Corporation, who also decided that the scheme should include a public convenience set below ground in a similar way to what was being done in London. By the autumn of 1894 it would seem that the shelter had finally been erected in a position near to the top of West Stockwell Street, seemingly all ready for the cabmen to take possession. However, nearly three months later, in January 1895, the shelter remained unoccupied. While the cabmen of the town were apparently eager to make use of the shelter, they felt that it lacked certain amenities such as heating, lighting and facilities to make tea and coffee, and thus the shelter remained empty. And so it continued for several months until finally in July 1895, with the town's cabmen still refusing to make use of the shelter, it was finally dismantled and later removed to the site of the present golf club, which was adjacent to Councillor Mackensie's home at 'Achnacone' in Bergholt Road, Braiswick.

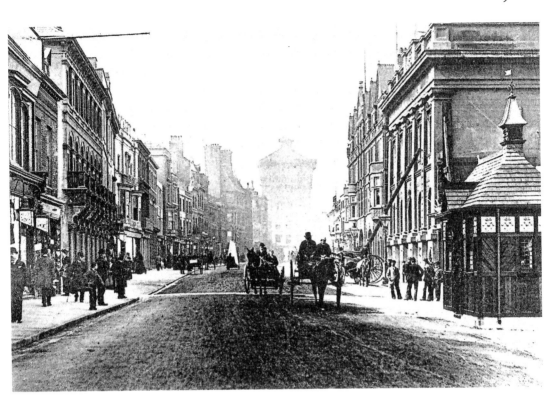

Above: This rare photograph of the High Street, dating from the early months of 1895, shows the cab shelter on the extreme right of the picture during the brief period that it remained there.

Right: Interior view of the old cab shelter as seen in 2017.

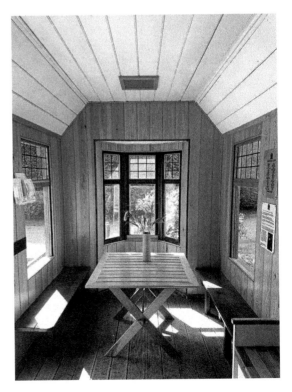

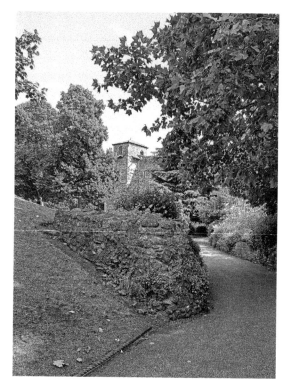

Left: This rather innocent-looking section of stone wall in Castle Park, which most people would probably pass by without giving a second glance, has an interesting story to tell. It is the only surviving section – standing above ground at least – of what was once part of the great curtain wall that surrounded the Temple of Claudius. The temple itself stood on the site of the Norman castle, which can be seen in the background.

Below: A reconstruction drawing of Roman Colchester by Peter Froste showing the position of the surviving fragment of stone wall in relation to the temple precinct and also the site of the Roman house foundations on view in Castle Park.

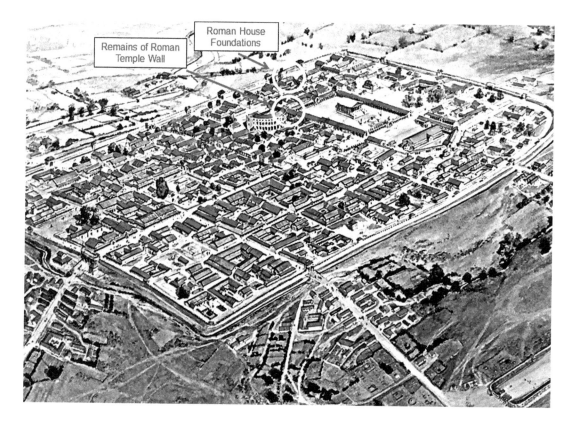

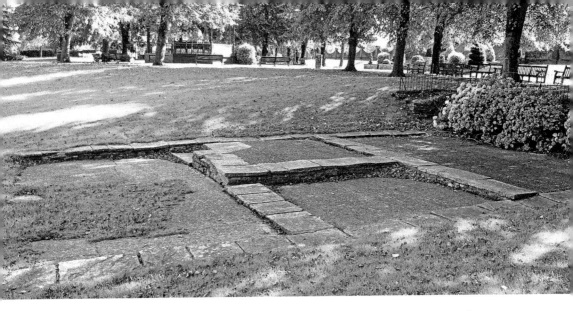

Just a short walk away from the above section of Roman wall, more Roman remains can be seen in the form of some first- or second-century house foundations that were excavated by the renowned archaeologist Sir Mortimer Wheeler in 1920. The foundations on display show part of a house that contained at least seven rooms and was flanked on its east side by two other buildings (running beneath the present bandstand), which appear to have been larger structures with their rooms surrounding open courtyards. Among the numerous finds discovered at the time were remains of mosaic and tessellated floors, coloured wall plaster and warm air heating hypocaust bricks – all suggestive of fairly wealthy occupants.

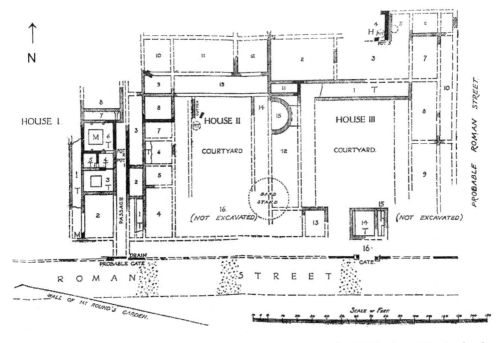

A plan of the excavations of the three houses produced in a report by Sir Mortimer Wheeler for the Morant Club in 1921. The remains that are visible today form part of the building seen on the left of the plan.

Acknowledgements

I would like to thank the following individuals and organisations for their valued help in compiling this book: John Burgess, Geoff Crick, Philip Crummy, Wayne Dutnell, Peter Froste, Andrea Hitchcock, Jess Jephcott, Justin Knight, Keith & Margaret Moss, Bruce Neville, Andrew Phillips, Bernard Polley, Peter Sansom and Gladys Rudd.

I would also like to mention my debt to the late John Bensusan Butt, whose excellent biographical indexes of Colchester people and buildings (recently edited and published by Shani D'Cruze) have proved to be a mine of information. My thanks are also due to Fred Nash (Essex County Council) for his articles and research relating to the Second World War defences of Colchester; to the staff of Bourne Pond Mill for allowing me access to take photographs of the site; to Colchester Golf Club for allowing me access to photograph the old cabmen's shelter; to the Colchester Archaeological Trust for permission to include a reconstruction drawing of Roman Colchester by Peter Froste; and to Colchester and Ipswich Museums for granting me permission to include a picture of an old Eryngo box that is in their collection.

Finally, my thanks are due to both Sareena Cobden and Amanda Francis for allowing me free access to the archive material maintained by the Winsley's Almshouses Charity Trust.

Also available from Amberley Publishing

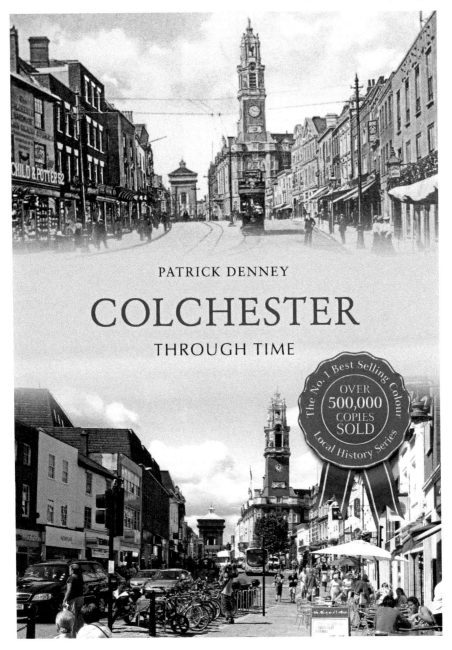

PATRICK DENNEY

COLCHESTER

THROUGH TIME

The No. 1 Best Selling Colour Local History Series

OVER
500,000
COPIES
SOLD

This fascinating selection of photographs traces some of the many ways in
which Colchester has changed and developed over the last century.

97818 48685 468

Available to order direct 01453 847 800

www.amberley-books.com

Also available from Amberley Publishing

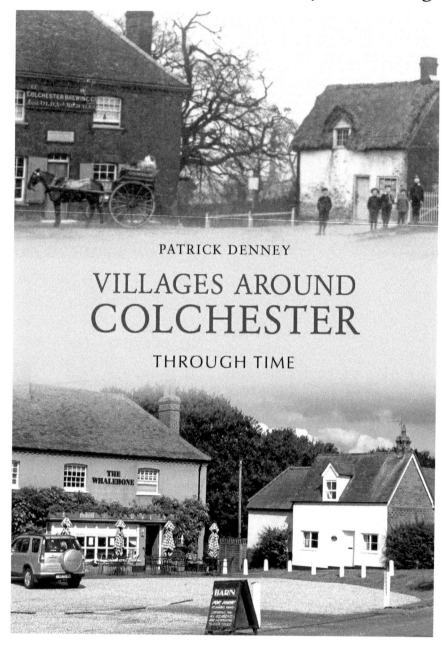

PATRICK DENNEY

VILLAGES AROUND
COLCHESTER

THROUGH TIME

This fascinating selection of photographs traces some of the many ways
in which the villages around Colchester have changed and developed
over the last century.

97818 48685 666

Available to order direct 01453 847 800

www.amberley-books.com